HAWAII: *Fiftieth Star*

To

JAMES A. MICHENER

author, thinker, friend of Hawaii, and
friend of mine

**THIS BOOK CONTAINS THE COMPLETE TEXT
OF THE ORIGINAL HARDBOUND EDITION**

Mutual Publishing
1127 11th Ave.
Honolulu, Hawaii 96816
Tel. (808) 732-1709 Fax (808) 734-4094

HAWAII: *Fiftieth Star*

by

A. GROVE DAY

Illustrated by JOHN V. MORRIS

Mutual Publishing • Honolulu, Hawaii

Contents

The Voyagers Find a Home

Volcanoes roared deep under the ocean. From cracks in the floor of the world's largest body of water, hot lava spurted forth.

This went on for millions of years.

A chain of mountains began to rise from the bottom of the Pacific, along cracks stretching for about a thousand miles from northwest to southeast. Closer and closer to the ocean's surface they rose.

Some of the mountains climbed into the sunshine and air. The tops smoked and spouted. Lava streamed down the slopes and into the water, where giant clouds of steam shot into the air. Islands were born.

The islands continued to grow through centuries. Every flow of lava made each island an inch or so higher. Some of

3

these volcanic islands grew very high, and in between erup-
tions the volcano tops would be powdered with snow. One
island finally rose about two miles above sea level, and another's peaks were almost three miles high!

Rain fell on the rocks, and the mountain domes were slowly
undercut and eroded. Plants, drifting to the shore or carried
as seeds by birds, took hold on the crumbling lava soil. The
slopes were colored with green and brown foliage.

The northwestern islands of the chain stopped smoking and
erupting. Their edges, gnawed by smashing waves, crumbled
and broke into ragged cliffs. The islands of the southeast,
though, still kept on building themselves, amid fiery fountains and drifting ashes.

And still, for thousands of years, no animals except a few
far-wandering birds saw these islands, which are among the
most isolated on the face of the earth.

Then, from the south, came the first men to live in this
group of islands that nowadays we call Hawaii, the Fiftieth
State.

The forefathers of the Hawaiians were a sailor race coming
from southern Asia centuries ago. They had dark skins, heavy
features, and dark wavy hair, but were of Caucasian stock.
They were the best seamen in the world at that time. When
sailors of Europe were still hugging the shores of their narrow
seas, the "vikings of the Pacific" were spreading eastward from
Asia over thousands of sea miles. They discovered and popu-
lated the inhabited islands within a vast area now called the
"Polynesian triangle." These people were later given the name
of Polynesians, from two Greek words meaning "many islands." And truly they were the greatest island-finders the
world has ever known.

Over many generations the Polynesians spread eastward,
probably by way of the hundreds of small islands now called

Micronesia. Some of these people settled around the lovely bays and valleys of Tahiti, in the South Pacific. From here, about the eighth century A.D., at least one canoeload of Polynesians must have gone north and discovered the chain of islands formed by volcanic action over the ages.

We do not know the name of the Polynesian Columbus who first sighted these isles. But to the biggest of them he gave a Polynesian name, Hawaii. A word similar to this had been used by other Polynesians to mean "home place," "heaven," or "Eden." Thus, the Hawaiian Islands, often called the "Paradise of the Pacific," got their name literally from a native word for "paradise."

The Polynesians used canoes made of hollowed-out logs, which were fitted with outriggers, or framework floats, to keep them steady on the waves. The canoes had sails of woven coconut or pandanus fiber. For long voyages they used two canoes, lashed together with flooring between the two hulls, on which shelters were built to protect their supplies.

How did these early navigators, who did not know about the needle compass, find their way around the vast Pacific? They guided their craft by the sun, the clouds over land, the wind on their cheeks, and the direction of waves and currents. They followed the sky tracks of birds. Mainly they traveled by the stars. The Polynesian helmsman knew more than a hundred and fifty stars by name. He could follow their changes and learn his latitude from them.

On a voyage of migration, when Polynesians set out to find homes in an ocean where they could not even be sure that any new islands existed, hundred-foot double canoes were used. From sixty to a hundred persons could live for weeks on such a vessel. The voyage from Tahiti would cover twenty-five hundred miles; yet we know that canoes using only sails and paddle power made this journey many times.

Such a canoe could sail as much as a hundred miles a day with a good wind. The crew was trained to live for a month without touching land if necessary. On the voyage that discovered Hawaii, women and children were probably taken along. Live animals—pigs, dogs, and chickens—were carried for use as food. Seeds and plant cuttings were also brought to the Islands by canoe—the coco palm, the banana, and the breadfruit trees must have been taken to Hawaii by human beings.

After their fresh stores were eaten, the seafarers could live for weeks on dried foods—pandanus flour, cooked breadfruit and sweet potatoes, preserved fish and shellfish. The voyagers also caught fish and cooked them on a bed of sand in the bottom of the canoe. Drinking water was carried in gourds or in bamboo pipes.

Yet the early canoe voyages were not luxury cruises. Perhaps more than one shipload of Polynesian venturers perished in storm or wreck, or died mad with thirst without catching a glimpse of the snow-capped mountains looming above the promised land of Hawaii.

The first settlers must have been delighted with the empty, free land they had found, where the trade winds brought coolness and the rains fell over green regions where taro could be grown. They sent back canoes with messages to friends and relatives. Others came north from Tahiti, and for several centuries there was traffic back and forth over the sea. But then the voyaging stopped for some reason, and for other centuries, until Captain James Cook and his two ships arrived in 1778, the Hawaiians were isolated. They had time to develop their own country and culture.

The island population grew, and rival chiefs fought to gain and hold petty domains. The larger islands—called Hawaii,

Maui, Oahu, and Kauai—were often held as "kingdoms" by families of strong chiefs.

At the top of the social scale were the *alii*, chiefs or nobles, who were warriors and lived off the produce of the common people. One's rank was inherited, and women as well as men could hold high positions. The chiefs were attended by councilors, by taxgatherers and stewards, and by the kahuna class. The kahunas were priests or specialists in various arts such as foretelling the future, locating spots for temples, supervising housebuilding and canoe making, predicting the weather, and curing the sick. They might also work magic spells or "pray a person to death."

The mass of the people were farmers, fishermen, canoe builders, birdcatchers, and the like. They depended on the *alii* class for protection, and served as soldiers during times of fighting. They also supplied the chiefs and their followers with food and other gifts. Taxes could be paid to the *alii* in hogs, dogs, fish nets, feathers, and sheets of cloth made of beaten bark. The chief could call out any of his people for labor. Usually the worker, as part of the rent for his land— the chief was supposed to own all the land—worked in his lord's fields one day out of five.

The laborer was not tied to the land, and could leave a cruel chief if he wished. Altogether, the lot of the ordinary man was probably better than that of the European peasant of the same period.

There were rules for the use of land and water, and there were primitive courts of justice. Robbery, especially of the goods of a chief, was a crime, often punished by death. But in times of war, rules and courts were forgotten and outlaw gangs roamed about.

There was one old custom that still survives in spirit in the Islands. "Hawaiian hospitality" was not merely a polite phrase.

A man of ancient Hawaii who let a stranger depart hungry from his door would suffer public shame. Houses were never locked in those days. While the family was away, they expected other travelers to stop in and partake of the food and water left in their thatched home for that purpose.

Questioning a stranger about where he had come from, where he was going, and whether he would return was not considered idle curiosity. The questioner wanted the privilege of entertaining the stranger. If one household had a visitor, a neighbor would soon drop in to find out how long he would remain. The entire village then rallied to entertain him, and food would appear on the table throughout his stay. Usually a field of taro and vegetables was cultivated by the village in common, and any family could draw upon this supply when a visitor arrived or some other special need arose.

When crops were abundant, a household was likely to have a flood of visitors, and those who came were considered foolish if they left while their hosts' food supply held out. Guests were expected to carry away with them all the remains of a feast. Otherwise it would seem that they were not satisfied with the fare.

The Hawaiians followed the Polynesian religion. It was a form of nature worship. A Supreme Being was supposed to rule the universe, but there were many other gods—one old chant mentions no fewer than four hundred thousand of them—that could be invoked.

The Polynesian gods most widely worshiped in Hawaii were four. Kane, father of living creatures, was identified with sunlight, fresh water, and the forests. Ku was the fierce god of war, to whom human sacrifices were sometimes made. Kaneloa ruled the land of departed spirits. Lono was the god of growing things, of rain, harvest, sports, and peace, during whose autumn *makahiki* festival a truce from war was joyously celebrated. A fifth, Pele, goddess of the volcanoes, was respected and feared, especially in the southeastern islands where fire still smoldered and burst forth from underground.

Certain gods were patrons of particular acts. Hina presided over women's work, Laka was goddess of the hula-dance schools, and Kuula was the god of fishermen. Some men were supposed to have gods as ancestors in their family tree. The Hawaiians also believed in legendary heroes, ghosts, and imps that could belong to a wizard. Rocks, plants, animals, stars, and other natural objects might at times be considered as divine beings.

Each family had an ancestral spirit—often in the form of an animal or fish—that was worshiped at the family altar. The main public worship was held on an enclosed temple platform called a heiau, decorated with large carved images of grinning gods. But every act of Hawaiian life, from the chopping of a tree to the planning of a war, was begun with a prayer or religious ceremony.

Two main ideas stand out in Hawaiian religion: "mana" and "*kapu.*" Mana is the supernormal power that may be possessed by a person or a thing. A man endowed with mana, which he could gain in several ways, might perform superhuman feats of courage, skill, or magic.

It was thought that contact between persons or objects with different amounts of mana could be dangerous to the weaker one. To control the handling of this power, many prohibitions grew up in the Hawaiian community. This was called the *kapu* system (the word *kapu* is the same as the word "tabu," used in other parts of Polynesia).

The idea of *kapu* grew out of a view of nature that divided everything into two parts or aspects. On one side everything was placed that was considered sacred—the male principle, light, life; on the other was placed that which was unsacred

—the female principle, darkness, and death. Whatever was branded as *kapu* was forbidden, either because it was divine and therefore to be set aside from what was vulgar and common, or else because it was corrupt, and thus dangerous to both the common and the divine.

Anything connected with the gods was sacred; hence there were many *kapus* relating to priests, temples, and worship. Since the noble class was supposed to have descended from the gods, the *alii*, particularly the highest ones, who had acquired much mana by birth, were protected by many *kapus*. Should a chief's shadow fall on a commoner, for example, it might mean death for him. In turn, the *alii* had to observe some *kapus* of their own.

Women, as allied with the negative principle, suffered under many rules. For instance, in the old days they could not eat pork, coconuts, or bananas.

Some *kapus* might be brief; others might last as long as thirty years. During a season of strict *kapu*, all lights and fires in the village would be put out; no one could bathe or go in a canoe; and everyone had to stay indoors. Even the animals had to keep quiet; dogs and hogs were muzzled, and chickens were hidden under a calabash.

Penalties for breaking a strong *kapu* were severe—quite often death. Ignorance of a *kapu* was no excuse. A person could break it without knowing, but had to pay the penalty anyway.

It became easy for the chiefs and priests to use the *kapu* system to govern the rest of the people. They were tempted to think up powerful prohibitions in order to make their rule secure. The system weighed heaviest upon the common people and upon women of all classes. It helped to hold the native society together, but through the years it was often misused.

The *kapu* system was one of the first of the old customs to be cast aside. After the Islands were united under one king and the people had been exposed to a generation of contact with white men, the old religion with its thou-shalt-nots was overthrown.

Daily Life in Old Hawaii

What was it like to live in the Islands in the old days?

Life was not easy then, but the natives were clever in using the things they had, to keep themselves alive and happy.

The early Hawaiians, unlike their luckier cousins in the islands to the south of them, had to work hard to grow their food.

Some of the crops were raised on grassy uplands or in forest clearings, where there was plenty of rain. To grow food in the lowlands, where their main crop, taro, needed plenty of water, the Hawaiians were smart. They irrigated by means of dams, tunnels, ditches, and bamboo pipes. The supply of water was shared by the farmers through a system of water rights.

Few tools were used by the farmer. The main one was the

o-o, a sharpened stick six to nine feet long, used for digging holes. Most of the backbreaking labor of tilling the soil was done with his bare hands. The taro farmer usually had to work in mud up to his waist. Wisely, he often worked all night in cool moonlight and rested in the heat of the day. This custom later led to charges by foreigners that the Hawaiian was lazy. The foreigner did not know he had often labored all night.

Poi, the Hawaiian staff of life, which is still eaten today, is made from the starchy root of the taro plant. The chief variety was grown in prepared beds with raised borders, so that the roots were always covered with water. The farmer planted at various times so that some taro was ripe during each month. Since the beds were used over and over, it was necessary to renew the soil by covering it with rotted leaves, weed mulch, and burned bones.

Sweet potatoes were set out in hills on the drier uplands. Bananas and sugar cane were planted from cuttings. Gourds were raised from seed in cleared ground, and calabash gourds could be grown in various useful shapes for making jugs and bowls. The paper mulberry tree from which bark cloth was made was planted in clumps near the villages.

The ancient Hawaiians did not live in fortified districts or large towns. Their villages clustered by the seashore or near their fields. The climate was so mild that they did not need much protection from sun or cold, but in some places heavy rains made a good roof necessary.

Captain Cook, the English discoverer of Hawaii, described the village of Waimea, on the island of Kauai, as a collection of thatched dwellings, large and small, scattered without any order, looking like English haystacks, with peaked roofs running almost to the ground. He thought them stuffy and poorly suited to the climate, but admitted that they were kept very clean, with floors covered with dry grass over which mats were spread for sleeping.

When a Hawaiian needed a house, there were no carpenters to make it for him. He had to do it himself with the aid of his friends. On a smooth stone platform, a notched frame of forest timbers and rafters was lashed together with cords of coconut fiber or rootlets of the ie vine. Even had there been metal nails in old Hawaii, this lashing would have been preferable, to hold the frame together in a high wind. The roof was thatched with a kind of grass, or else with leaves of sugar cane or the ti plant. The thatching was tied in bundles and lashed to crosspieces in the roof frame. This roof would last for five to ten years.

Instead of building a large house with many rooms, the Hawaiians liked to build several small houses near each other. A simple farm might have one or two huts and a storehouse. A chief might have six or seven little houses. These would be an eating house for the men, an eating house for the women, a work shelter for the women, a sleeping house, and a retreat for women only. There might also be a small stone platform to hold the family altar, and a shed on the shore to cover the canoe. Everything was kept spotlessly clean. A Hawaiian village in the early days was swept daily with a broom of coco-palm branches.

Fire was a great danger to the thatched houses. The cooking ovens were removed from the rest of the home places. Strange to say, the men of old Hawaii not only provided the food but cooked it as well. Since men and women were not allowed to eat together, the men had to cook two meals, one for the women and one for themselves. Moreover, the menu was different, for many things were *kapu* for the women to eat.

The Hawaiians did not often eat meat. Such food came

only from pigs, chickens and wild birds, and dogs. Dogs were considered quite a delicacy and were fattened in cages before a feast. Vegetables included baked breadfruit, sweet potatoes and yams, bananas, arrowroot, sugar cane, and greens such as cooked taro tops. For relishes they had salt gathered from pools by the shore, roasted candlenuts, dried octopus, and a seaweed called limu. The main foods were fish and poi.

Preparing the daily poi was hard work. The root had to be steamed for hours in an underground oven, to break up the tiny, sharp crystals that otherwise would cut one's tongue. The root was then peeled and pounded into a thick paste. This was done on a scooped-out "poi board" with a flat-bottomed stone called a poi pounder. Then the paste was mixed with water to the proper stiffness—"one-finger poi" is thicker than "three-finger poi." The food was served in large calabashes, and everyone ate from the common supply, dipping his fingers into the bowl. Poi dough could be dried out and kept for weeks. When needed, it was moistened and pounded into a paste.

Food could be boiled in a calabash of water by the process of dropping red-hot stones into it. The main method of cooking, though, was baking in a hole in the ground. Stones were laid over an open fire which had been burning for some time in the pit. The hot stones were then covered with grass on which the food was spread, bundled up in leaves. Then the whole mass was covered with green leaves and old mats and banked with earth. The food steamed for hours until it was taken out and served. This delicious Hawaiian barbecue was called a *luau.*

Taro required three or four hours to bake; the rest of the food was put in much later than the taro. A whole pig could be cooked in the pit. Hot stones were put inside the body so that the meat would be thoroughly done. Puddings of coconut, sugar, and arrowroot were baked in packages made of ti leaves.

The menu was varied by many kinds of seafood, including oysters, lobsters, and crabs. Certain fish, such as mullet, were caught and fattened in rock-walled ponds along the shore The fish were broiled over coals, or steamed in ti leaves, or boiled in a calabash with hot stones. Sometimes the fish were salted and dried in the sun for future eating.

The meal was spread outdoors in good weather. Food was cooked for several days ahead, and was usually eaten cold. The diners reclined around clean mats, decorated with ferns and flowers, on which the meal was laid out. After everyone had dipped his fill in the same calabashes as the others, he would daintily wash in a fingerbowl. All scraps were kept and carefully burned afterward.

Meals were times of gaiety and cheerful conversation. Nothing serious was discussed at table. In the middle of a meal the diners might enjoy getting a relaxing lomi-lomi, or native massage. Often they were entertained by songs or recitals of the deeds of their great ancestors.

No fixed times were set for eating. If food was plentiful, the people might eat five or six meals a day, rising in the middle of the night for a snack. If food was scarce, the people might go for two or three days without eating, and then have a feast.

The houses were furnished with many utensils made and decorated by the people. Lovely circular bowls of various sizes were carved from blocks of seasoned hardwood. Ring-shaped mats were put under the bowls to keep them from tipping. Large dishes and platters were also carved of wood. Dippers, spoons, and cups were made of coconut shells. Clothing, featherwork, and fishing gear were stowed in large gourds with lids. Only a few dishes were made of stone, but taro and seaweed and other herbs were pounded in a mortar.

Slop basins and spittoons were important, for it was believed that if a wizard could obtain a person's spittle or fingernail parings, these might be used to "pray him to death." The chiefs kept trusted servants who would collect and secretly bury this refuse.

Fire was kindled with a Polynesian invention, the "fire plow." A slender hardwood stick was rubbed back and forth in a groove on a softer piece of wood on the ground. The smoldering dust was fanned on a bit of bark cloth until this tinder burst into flame.

At night, torches were used. These were made of dried candlenut kernels, wrapped in leaves and tied to a bamboo pole. Indoors, candles made of these oily kernels strung on a stick were used, or else a stone lamp fitted with candlenut oil and a twisted wick.

The Stone Age craftsman of Hawaii lacked any metals but had an amazing skill in working with tools of stone, shell, wood, and bone. His chief tool was a stone adz, like an ax head tied to a handle. These varied in size from one more than a foot long, with which to chop down a tree, to tiny ones an inch long. Hammers and chisels were also made of stone. Knives were made of wooden blades on which shark's teeth were tied. Awls and scrapers were formed of shells, and files were made of sharp-edged coral. Needles of bone were used in sewing together the edges of sheets of bark cloth for bedclothes. A clever rotary drill, with a point of stone, was used for boring holes.

Woman's work in the old days included the rearing of children, the plaiting of mats, and the making of bedcovers and clothing from the inner bark of the paper mulberry tree. This material was peeled off, soaked in water, scraped, and then beaten into thin strips, which were overlapped to make wider pieces, and built up into layers for thickness. This cloth was called kapa. The musical sound of the kapa mallet beating on a wooden anvil was a homelike noise in the Hawaiian village.

The mallet was a square-edged club on which grooves or patterns were cut, which gave different textures to the surface of the cloth. The fabric was bleached in the sun or dyed in various colors. On it designs were stamped with carved bamboo sticks, used as in block printing.

The Hawaiians wore few clothes. The man's loincloth, or malo, was made of kapa. He wound it around his waist and tucked the end between his legs. The woman wore a short kapa skirt called a *pa-u*. In the evening, either the man or woman might wear a square shawl called a *kihei*. Kapa clothing might be soaked in coconut oil to make it waterproof; raincoats of matting were also worn. But kapa could not be laundered and did not last very long under heavy wear.

Styles had to be followed, and a commoner risked death if he donned the malo of a chief. Ladies of high rank wore skirts with many decorations. They wrapped several lengths of kapa around and around their waists.

Few people ever were so skilled as the Hawaiians in featherwork. Their helmets and cloaks, made from the tufts of feathers of thousands of birds, were worn only by chiefs. A special group of birdcatchers went into the dense forests and trapped their prey on twigs smeared with a sticky gum. Each bird had one or two yellow or red feathers, and these only were plucked. The bird was then released to grow new ones. Birds were also caught alive with light nets of fiber, with nooses, and even with the bare hands when they had been attracted by imitations of their calls.

When making cloaks and capes, a netting of fiber was

woven, to which the feathers were carefully tied. Patterns of geometric figures were made in contrasting colors of yellow and red, with now and then a touch of black. Some cloaks were nine feet across and six feet long, and at least one of them now in a museum used no less than eighty thousand feathers!

With his cloak the *alii* wore a helmet of ie fibers on which were tied hundreds of bright feathers. Most of these helmets had a raised crest and in design somewhat resembled those of Greek warriors or knights of old Europe.

A nobleman's followers carried his kahili, a tall pole decorated with feathers. The poles were made of carved wood or of the bones of defeated chiefs.

Both men and women were fond of adorning themselves with shell bracelets, with pendants of boar's tusks, and with anklets made of hundreds of teeth from dogs. Some Hawaiians decorated their bodies with tattoo marks.

The favorite adornment was the *lei*, a necklace or headband made of various kinds of material. Giving a *lei* is still the symbol of love and friendship in Hawaii. It was made of flowers, leaves, or ferns strung into a garland. But *leis* were also made of carved dried candlenuts, of shells, of seeds, of beads carved from walrus tusks, and of bright feathers. The most treasured ornament was a whale's tooth, carved in the form of a hook and hung on many fine strings of braided human hair.

The Hawaiians did not know how to weave on a loom, but were very good at braiding fiber to make mats, baskets, rope, and fishing lines.

They did not walk much around their islands, but traveled mostly by sea. Their canoes were truly works of art. These varied in size from a one-man outrigger for fishing to large double canoes for voyaging to neighboring islands. The outrigger was a long wooden float lashed on one side of the canoe to keep the craft from overturning. Planks were fastened above the canoe hulls to keep out the waves, and stem and stern were covered.

Paddles were four or five feet long. Chiefs kept crews of hefty sailors who did nothing but handle the hundred-foot war canoes. Some canoes had triangular sails of woven matting, and were guided by a long steering oar.

The old Hawaiians spent many hours in outdoor sports. About three months in the autumn were devoted to a festival called the *makahiki*, a period of peace dedicated to the god Lono. Thousands of persons would gather to watch bouts of boxing, wrestling, bowling, and javelin throwing. A popular sport was a sort of summertime toboggan ride on a downhill course paved with stones and grass. The daring riders balanced on a sled with narrow runners, and often narrowly avoided a bad tumble.

Most popular of all were water sports. The Hawaiians spent many hours in the surf. Canoe-racing, swimming, diving, body-surfing, and surfboard-riding were the most favored diversions. Riding the waves while standing erect on a sliding wooden board was the great pastime of chiefs and kings.

When the first ships of the white men sighted Hawaii, they were greeted by natives who came out swimming or paddling their canoes. In this way the Stone Age people welcomed Captain Cook, who first brought news of Hawaii to the outside world.

The Death of the Discoverer

THE MAN WHO REVEALED THE HAWAIIAN ISLANDS TO THE rest of the nations was the greatest sailor of his time. But when the Hawaiians decided that this man must behave like a god, his doom was set.

This discoverer was Captain James Cook, who had been born on another island, England, far on the other side of the world from Hawaii. He was a handsome and modest man about fifty years old when he found the new archipelago. Then at the height of his fame, he did not dream that his actions were to lead to a tragedy.

Even during his boyhood on a small farm, James Cook had yearned to become a sailor. He left home and got a place on a North Sea sailing vessel that hauled coal. When England went to war with the French in 1755, James entered the

British Navy. After many years of hard work he became the most skilled navigator in the world.

An early attempt to solve the mysteries of space first sent Captain Cook to the Pacific. Astronomers wanted to go to the South Seas in 1768 because from Tahiti they could best view a rare sight—the passing of the planet Venus in front of the sun's face. Cook headed the expedition, and did so well that for the next ten years his life was devoted to making Pacific discoveries and writing about his finds.

Even a war was not allowed to hinder the progress of James Cook's great work. When in 1776 he set out on his third voyage to the Pacific, Benjamin Franklin and the American Continental Congress sent out orders to their ships not to attack Captain Cook. He was not an enemy but a world scientist.

Toward the end of 1777, Captain Cook with his two ships, the *Resolution* and the *Discovery*, was sailing in the Pacific, headed in the direction of the North Pole. He had orders to seek the fabled Northwest Passage, a strait which everybody hoped would be found, connecting the Pacific Ocean with the North Atlantic. Cook never found the passage, but he did stumble upon a group of islands which today are the Fiftieth State.

Neither Cook nor anybody else from Europe had any reason to suspect that there was anything but empty ocean north of Tahiti. Thus Cook had a right to be excited when in January, 1778, he wrote in his journal: "In the morning of the 18th, an island made its appearance, bearing northeast by east; and soon after, we saw more land, bearing north, and entirely detached from the former. . . . On the 19th, at sunrise, the island first seen bore east, several leagues distant. I stood for the other, which we could reach; and not long after, discovered a third island, in the direction of west-northwest."

These were Oahu, Kauai, and little Niihau, some of the beautiful islands of the Hawaiian chain.

Off Kauai, many canoes came to Cook's ships. The people greeted him in a language that he could partly understand, for it was very much like the tongue he had learned in Tahiti. The Hawaiians at first feared to leave their canoes and come aboard. Captain Cook himself, at the rail of the *Resolution*, tied some brass medals to a rope and dangled them overside. The brown-skinned men grinned, took the medals, and tied some small fish on the line. They knew how to barter one thing for another! That was the beginning of trade between the Hawaiians, in their brightly colored loincloths, and the white strangers in their British clothes and three-cornered hats.

These Stone Age people were eager to get pieces of iron, which they had never owned before. For some small nails, which they needed to make fishhooks, they offered more fish and one of the big yams for which Kauai was to become famous. One of the men even offered to trade his kapa malo from around his waist. Later Captain Cook found that for a medium-sized nail he could get enough pork to supply his whole crew for a day, and plenty of potatoes for a small nail.

Soon the natives overcame their fears and came aboard, after first praying to their gods. Then, on deck, they "sang and made motions with their hands," greeting Captain Cook with a hula dance.

The Hawaiians soon made it clear that they had never seen such vessels or people before. They thought the ships were floating islands, and the masts were trees.

Sad to say, they soon found out that the strangers had iron tubes that could make a loud noise and kill people from a distance. The officer of a boat sent to look for an anchorage became frightened when the natives lifted the entire boat and its crew ashore as a friendly gesture. He fired at one of the

Hawaiians, who was carried, dying, into the woods. Captain Cook was angry that this first encounter with a strange people should have ended in bloodshed.

That afternoon Captain Cook went ashore at the village of Waimea. The throng of Hawaiians fell down on their faces, the way they did to honor their highest chiefs. This stranger from over the sea must be a demigod at least! Thereafter, Captain Cook was followed by an admiring crowd who watched his every act.

After a few days at Kauai, the two ships sailed across the channel to the islet of Niihau, where Cook traded for yams and salt. In return he gave the people some goats, which they had never seen before, and some melon, pumpkin, and onion seeds to plant.

After two weeks, Captain Cook sailed away from the group, which he had christened the Sandwich Islands in honor of the fourth Earl of Sandwich, his patron at the British Admiralty. But although Cook beat his way up the American coast to Alaska and then over to Asia, he did not find the legendary Northwest Passage. As the Arctic winter came on, he remembered with joy the warm region he had discovered, and headed back to the Sandwich Islands.

During the ten months since he had visited Kauai, the news of Cook's visit had spread through the group to islands which Cook had not yet seen. The Hawaiians, after much thought, had decided who he was.

Once, ran the legend, there was a King of Hawaii named Lono. He had killed his wife in a fit of anger, and then gone mad with grief. He had wandered through all the Islands, boxing and wrestling with anyone he met. Then he had set out, in an odd-shaped big canoe, for foreign lands. His people had made him a god, in whose honor annual games were held in the season of *makahiki*, or harvest. During the celebration the priests marched around with banners on poles with crosspieces. Now, again in the *makahiki* season, Cook's ships reappeared in Hawaiian waters, their sails looking much like the procession banners of Lono. As the ships cruised slowly along the island shores, the people on the beaches hailed Captain Cook as Lono, come back again to his land.

On the morning of November 26, 1778, Cook's ships found themselves off the north coast of the island of Maui. "In the middle of the country," Cook wrote, "was an elevated saddle hill, whose summit appeared above the clouds." This hill, as he called it, was the mighty mass of Haleakala, "The House of the Sun," ten thousand feet high, the largest dormant volcano crater on earth. Later in the day the strangers caught a glimpse of the island of Molokai.

The King of Maui had heard about these people whose loosely fitting skins (their European clothing) held pockets from which they could pull out wonderful gifts. They spoke in a strange babble, he was told, and smoke came out of their mouths. He went out to the *Discovery* and presented the captain with a rich cloak made from thousands of bird feathers.

A few days later, off the east end of Maui, King Kalaniopuu, the old ruler of the island of Hawaii to the south, who was at the time fighting a war on Maui, came to visit the *Resolution* and make friends with Captain Cook. Some of the chiefs with him stayed overnight. One of them was the King's nephew, a husky young warrior who studied the strangers and their guns. His name was Kamehameha. Later the whole world was to hear about him.

Then for six weeks Cook's ships sailed around the south shores of the Big Island, as the island of Hawaii is called. Unfavorable winds kept them from landing anywhere, but the natives often came out for miles in their canoes to supply them with sugar cane, pork, and other provisions. As a special treat they offered the Englishmen a live, squirming octopus to eat.

Cook did not find a sheltered harbor until on January 17, 1779, the ships dropped anchor in Kealakekua Bay on the west side of the Big Island. Here ten thousand happy Hawaiians, shouting and singing, swam out to greet the newcomers, or else rode canoes and surfboards. Cook had never before seen such a crowd in the Pacific. No wonder that he now wrote in his journal that they had made a discovery "in many respects the most important that had hitherto been made by Europeans throughout the extent of the Pacific Ocean."

As soon as Cook went ashore, he was greeted by the Hawaiian priests as the returned god Lono. The British officer was led to the top of a rickety platform and there was wrapped in a red cloth and asked, by signs, to kiss one of the wooden images whose horrible faces grinned down on the scene. Cook agreed. It was the most dangerous step in his career. From now on, he must act not as a man, but as a god.

A week later, King Kalaniopuu returned from Maui and came out to renew his friendship. He presented Cook with several feather capes and a supply of hogs, coconuts, and breadfruit. In return he was given a linen shirt, Cook's own sword, and a complete tool chest.

Ashore there were Hawaiian exhibitions of boxing and wrestling in honor of Lono. Then Captain Cook gave the natives their first band concert and fireworks display.

After a pleasant fortnight, the ships were loaded with food and firewood, and were ready to continue their voyage. The farewell feast and final gift-giving were over, and on February 4 the two ships headed north. But a sudden storm hit them at midnight four days later, and events began to swing toward tragedy.

The foremast of the *Resolution* fell down, and the planking began to leak. The "floating islands" had to turn around and slink back to the harbor to refit.

The people were not so friendly now as before. They wondered why the white men had come back. But the mast was laid out ashore, with a marine guard camped nearby to protect the carpenters and sailmakers at their work.

On the afternoon of Saturday, February 13, there was a clash between a watering party ashore and several Hawaiian chiefs. Captain Cook hurried ashore and smoothed things over. But as he was starting back to the ship, he heard shots fired and saw a canoe heading toward the beach. The native in it had daringly stolen a pair of iron tongs and a chisel, and was trying to escape inland with this treasure.

A friendly Hawaiian named Palea got back the stolen goods, but he was hit over the head in a scuffle, and two hundred angry natives began throwing chunks of jagged lava rock at the boat's crew. Palea managed to keep order and sent the seamen back safely. But when Captain Cook, who had joined in the chase for the thief, returned to his ship, he was worried. This stealing must stop, or none of his precious equipment would be safe, and the ships would be crippled.

That night, though, despite a careful watch, the sailing cutter anchored under the *Discovery*'s bow was cunningly stolen and taken ashore. The natives planned to burn it up and salvage the nails that held it together.

Captain Cook decided he would have to teach the Hawaiians a lesson. His men were outnumbered a hundred to one. Their force was divided, and the mast was still ashore. Cook loaded both barrels of his gun, one with harmless bird shot, the other with deadly ball. He led a party of marines ashore.

The captain was going to try a trick he had used before in the Pacific with success. He was going to get the King on board his ship and hold him as a hostage until the stolen boat was returned.

At Kalaniopuu's house, Cook decided that the King did not know about the thefts. The King and his two young sons agreed to go aboard the ship. But on the way, the Queen became frightened and warned the party not to go further.

A crowd of suspicious natives gathered, waving clubs, spears, and iron daggers made by the ships' blacksmiths for trade with the Hawaiians. Now the daggers were to be turned against their makers.

Bad news arrived at that moment. One of Palea's brothers, trying to run the blockade set up by the Englishmen in the bay, had been killed by a bullet.

Women and children disappeared. Cook gave up his scheme, and decided to try to get his men safely to the beach and their boats. His retreat was almost cut off by the milling crowd of warriors, who began tying on armor of woven matting. None of these Hawaiians had ever seen a gun kill a man, and hence they were not afraid of the muskets of the marines.

The soldiers formed a line by the waterside, hoping to escape to the boats offshore. Palea's eldest brother tried to stab Cook with one of the iron daggers. Cook fired at him the charge of bird shot, which rattled harmlessly off the woven armor.

The natives grew bolder. Another one of them aimed a blow at Cook, who fired the second barrel. The man fell dead. The marines fired a volley, which was drowned out by the shrieks of the brown warriors. Then the attackers flowed down to the water's edge.

Four marines were killed. The rest scrambled into the waves and swam to a waiting boat. Captain Cook was left alone on the shore of the island he had discovered. He turned his back to the natives and shouted an order for the men in the boats to cease firing and come in closer to the rocky shore.

A club struck him down. As he tried to rise, a dagger was plunged into his back. The blood ran. He groaned. A god does not groan. A shout arose: "This is not the real Lono!"

Then Captain Cook's body was overwhelmed by the howling attackers who, snatching the dagger from each other's hands, savagely joined in the destruction of the chief of the white strangers.

The Rise of the Conqueror

UNDER MUSKET FIRE FROM THE BOATS, THE HAWAIIANS retreated, leaving some of their warriors dead but carrying the bodies of the slain Englishmen.

The remains of Captain Cook were honored like those of a native god. The body was divided, and each high chief was given a piece. The bones were cleaned and buried secretly. But after a week of useless fighting and bombardment from the ships' cannons against the defenseless villages, a truce was called. The Hawaiians returned some parts of Cook's body, which were placed in a wooden coffin, draped with a British flag, and buried deep in the waters of the bay.

Sadly, the two ships finally departed from Hawaii on the night of February 22 and sailed north, past the islands of Maui, Lanai, and Molokai. After visiting the north shore of

Oahu, they crossed to Kauai, site of their first contact with the Hawaiians. Then they stopped for water and provisions at Niihau. A civil war had lashed the land, and the goats and pigs left there the previous year had been eaten. On March 15 the two ships finally left the Sandwich group. More than six years were to pass before other "floating islands" would appear in Hawaiian waters.

During this period, one of the chiefs, who had spent many hours on Cook's ships, began his march to the conquest of the entire island chain. The kingdom that he was able to build was fated finally to become an American state.

This chief was Kamehameha, who became the national hero of the Hawaiian people. He had observed the fatal force of the white man's gunpowder during the fighting at Kealakekua Bay, in which he himself had been wounded. He decided that these new methods could be used to end the centuries of tribal warfare which had made the islands a battleground. The story of his rise to power, uniting all the islands under one king, is filled with drama and romance.

The story began at the court of the high chief of Kohala, the northernmost part of the island of Hawaii. One of the chief's stepsons had married a niece of the high chief of the island of Maui. On a stormy night in November a son was born to this couple. The year is not surely known, but perhaps it was 1758, for a bright star, which may have been Halley's comet, blazed at the birth.

The soothsayers of the ruler of Kohala had reported that the baby would grow up to be a rebel who would "slay the chiefs." Orders were given by this ruler, just as Herod in the Bible gave orders, to kill the child as soon as it was born. But the mother had made a plan, and the baby was at once taken away secretly and reared in the mountains by two faithful servants.

When the child was five, the chief relented and little Kamehameha—in the Hawaiian language his name means "The Lonely One"—was brought to the court and trained as a young prince. He was taught by a famous fighter, Kekuhaupio, to be a skilled warrior. When Kamehameha's uncle, Kalaniopuu—the King who had almost been kidnaped by Captain Cook—became high chief, the young soldier was already famed, and in battle had saved the life of his former tutor, Kekuhaupio. One of Kamehameha's foes once reported that he "could break the body of his opponent in twain, while poised on his spear in mid-air. This little man was of a hard, thickset build, with large lips."

By the time Cook's ships arrived, Kamehameha was a leader among the *alii*, or Hawaiian nobility. A year later, King Kalaniopuu held a council and proclaimed his son Kiwalao as heir to the kingdom. He also named Kamehameha to be the guardian of the image of the terrible war-god.

Kamehameha took his duties so seriously that he quarreled with the prince. Following the advice of the King he retired for a while to his lands by the sea, where he lived the life of a farmer, fisherman, and sportsman.

The death of the King in 1782 brought Kamehameha back to the wars. The young new King, Kiwalao, was under the thumb of an uncle who was trying to push everyone else out of the picture, and four of the other chiefs asked Kamehameha to join with them and resist this oppression. He did so and during the civil wars that followed, the five warriors became famous for their loyalty to each other as long as they lived.

During the next ten years, the group led by Kamehameha, with headquarters in the Kona region that Cook had visited, were pitted against the chiefs of all the rest of the main islands. One incident of the warring period has passed into legend. During a raid on the coast south of Hilo, Kamehameha leaped ashore to attack a few unarmed fishermen on the beach. His foot caught in a crack in the lava and, when he was thus held in a trap, one of the fishermen boldly struck him on the head with a canoe paddle, which shattered against his skull.

When Kamehameha's comrades came to free him, the fishermen escaped. Later they were caught, though, and brought before Kamehameha to be punished. The chief freely admitted that he had been wrong to attack innocent workers, and set them free with many gifts. Then he uttered a saying which is still remembered as the Law of the Splintered Paddle: "Let the aged men and women and little children lie down in safety in the road." Thereafter, he promised to punish anyone who harmed defenseless subjects.

Just before the attack on Captain Cook at Kealakekua Bay, Kamehameha had come on board the *Discovery* and traded his valuable red feather cloak for seven iron daggers. During the civil wars he was even more aware of the value of white men's weapons. He began collecting muskets and cannons, and hired a few wandering white men to fire them. The early trading vessels that came to Hawaii from many foreign lands, including the United States, could always sell guns and powder to Kamehameha.

In spite of the occasional fighting, the era of the rise of Kamehameha was as close as the Hawaiian people ever came to a golden age. The climate allowed the people to live outdoors most of the time, and they worked, played, and fought with energy and kept in healthy trim.

In most ways, the Islands were truly a paradise. There were no mosquitoes, cockroaches, scorpions, centipedes, house rats, or measles viruses to plague the population. All these pests were brought in by ships from overseas.

The foreigners did bring in many useful animals and plants, starting with Cook's goats and pumpkin seeds. But the arrival of more and more strangers, bringing new diseases and harmful customs, did much to cause the Hawaiian race almost to die out in the century and a half after its discovery. Cook figured that about three hundred thousand Hawaiians lived in the Islands. Today only about twelve thousand pure-blooded Hawaiians are to be found living in the state. However, a large number married people of other races, so that a goodly portion of the citizens of the Fiftieth State have the blood of Kamehameha's people in their veins.

It is possible that a few foreigners—Spanish or perhaps Japanese—had been shipwrecked on the islands before Cook arrived. But if they were, they made no impression on history, and it was left to the English to bring to the world the first accounts of Hawaii.

The first ships to arrive after Cook were those of several nations who had been trading for sea-otter furs with the Indians on the northwest coast of America. The crews soon discovered that Hawaii was a wonderful place to stop on their way to China, to get news and provisions and to rest during the winter season.

Most of the earliest visitors were British. The first American ship to arrive came in the fall of 1789, the year George Washington became president of the United States. It was called the *Columbia Rediviva* and went on to earn the fame of being the first American ship to sail around the world. During the next few years the trans-Pacific fur trade became almost an American monopoly.

The first Hawaiian to visit the United States was a young Kauai lad named Opai, who went around the world on the *Columbia Rediviva*. He came back to the Islands in 1791 on a ship commanded by Joseph Ingraham. Opai, in true Hawaiian fashion, had swapped names with the captain, and thereafter called himself "Joseph Ingraham."

The first French ship to visit Hawaii came in 1791 on a round-the-world voyage. In the same year the flag of Spain was seen in these waters on a ship going from Mexico to China.

The most celebrated foreigners who settled in Hawaii in the early days were two Britishers. Sailing in American ships, they were survivors of a tragic happening known as the *Fair American* massacre.

Early in 1791, a Boston vessel was trading with the Hawaiians off the island of Maui when one of its boats was stolen and the sailor in it was killed. The captain, Simon Metcalfe, got revenge by firing his cannons at the canoes of many natives that he had lured within range, and at least a hundred Hawaiians were killed. They did not forget, and their chief, who had been lashed by Metcalfe with a rope's end, promised them that the next foreign ship that came along would pay for the killing.

The next ship happened to be the little schooner *Fair American*, in charge of Captain Metcalfe's eighteen-year-old son Thomas. He arrived off the island of Hawaii a few weeks later, hoping to rejoin his father. The chief who sought revenge did not know that his enemy's son was on the *Fair American*—that was an unplanned irony. But the Hawaiians took the schooner unawares, threw poor Tom overboard to drown, and killed four other members of the crew.

The only one who survived was a man named Isaac Davis. He had been spared because he fought bravely. He was found tied in a canoe, half blind and half dead, by an American living ashore, who interceded for him and nursed him back to health.

Soon Davis met John Young, Captain Metcalfe's boatswain, who had been sent ashore down the Kona coast on the very day of the attack on the *Fair American* to see if he could get some news of young Tom from one of the Americans ashore. Chief Kamehameha had kept Young from returning to his ship to tell of the massacre, and Captain Metcalfe, lacking the news, finally sailed off without his boatswain and without his son.

Young and Davis were simple and uneducated sailors, but they were both men of common sense. Soon they became Kamehameha's most trusted advisers. Young was best known by his nickname Olohana (a Hawaiian version of his boatswain's cry, "All hands!"). He aided Kamehameha in the civil wars, and later became governor of several islands. He died in Honolulu in 1835. One of his granddaughters became the good Queen Emma. Isaac Davis, a Welshman, also became a high chief and founded the oldest foreign family in the Hawaiian Islands. The British obtained a high reputation with Kamehameha in the early days in large part because of the characters of these two Englishmen who helped Kamehameha to his throne.

Kamehameha, with the advice of such friendly foreigners, now started broader operations in his attempt to unite all the islands under his rule. In the spring of 1790 his army invaded Maui and fought a battle in the valley near Wailuku, under the green peak called the Iao Needle. The dead bodies filled the stream in such heaps that the battle was given a name in Hawaiian meaning "the damming of the waters."

After capturing Maui and Lanai, Kamehameha went on to the island of Molokai. Here he made a friendly pact with the highborn widow of King Kalaniopuu. He took the guardianship of her granddaughter, Keopuolani, and when the girl was old enough, Kamehameha married her and made her his "sacred wife," in this way allying himself with the highest blood of the land. Both their two sons were destined to follow Kamehameha I on the throne.

A famous oracle told Kamehameha that, if he wanted to make himself master of the whole Big Island, he should build a great new temple platform on the Kona coast in honor of the war-god. But before he could do so, he had to fight more battles. Young Keoua, stepbrother of Kiwalao, who ruled the southern part of Hawaii, had started another civil war. Keoua killed his uncle in the struggle, and then turned to battle against Kamehameha.

One day when Keoua was returning to his base after fighting in the Hilo region, his army was hit by a terror which everyone thought foretold even greater disaster.

They marched by a route that took them near the volcanic crater of Kilauea. While they camped nearby, a sudden and violent eruption began. The air was filled with smoke, ashes, rocks, and poisonous gas. Although they would have been safe if they had stayed in their camp, the warriors and their train of women and children became fearful and tried to escape. When one of the groups, about four hundred people, was passing just beyond the mouth of the crater, the earth exploded. The entire band died in their tracks, mostly by suffocation. The event was taken as an omen that Pele, the Hawaiian volcano goddess, was on the side of Kamehameha.

Kamehameha got busy at Kona, building the immense heiau, or temple, as the oracle had ordered. The priests directed thousands of common people, who came from all parts of the island, to carry stones. The chiefs and even Kamehameha himself hauled rocks with their own hands, to honor the war-god.

King Kahekili of Maui, who was the uncle of Kamehameha's mother, was also trying to extend his power over all the islands. With a large fleet of canoes he invaded northern Hawaii. Kamehameha's policy of collecting foreign guns and gunners now paid off. Some small cannon were mounted on double canoes, manned by crews under the direction of John

Young and Isaac Davis. Kamehameha also probably used the *Fair American* as a warship.

But Kahekili's fleet also had foreign gunners, and the sea battle off the northern coast was so long and bloody that it became known as "the battle of the red-mouthed gun." At last the cannons of Kamehameha drove the enemy back to Maui.

The great heiau was finished in the summer of 1791, and Kamehameha ordered Keoua to come and meet him there face to face. Fatalistically, Keoua agreed. As he was about to step out of his canoe, one of the companions of Kamehameha killed him with a spear. The young King's body was the first sacrifice on the altar of the war-god, and thus perished the last chief who stood in the way of Kamehameha's dominion over the entire great island of Hawaii.

The Wars of
Kamehameha the Great

THEREAFTER FOR SEVERAL YEARS, KAMEHAMEHA WAS CONTENT merely to rule over the Big Island. Captain George Vancouver, who had served as a midshipman under Cook, made three visits to the Sandwich Islands between 1792 and 1794. He found that Kamehameha had mellowed since Vancouver had first seen him fourteen years before.

"I was agreeably surprised," Vancouver wrote, "in finding that his riper years had softened that stern ferocity which his younger days had exhibited, and had changed his general deportment to an address characteristic of an open, cheerful, and sensible mind, combined with great generosity and goodness of disposition." He concluded that Kamehameha's conduct had been "of the most princely nature."

On the second of his three visits, Vancouver brought into

the Islands from California some cattle and sheep. These
animals were to be the beginning of a grazing industry that
later was to produce that dashing figure, the Hawaiian cowboy.

At first view of the cattle on Vancouver's ship, Kamehameha, who had never seen such big animals, feared they
might harm him. Later he began asking all sorts of questions
about their care and feeding. When the first cow was taken
ashore at Kealakekua Bay, she dashed wildly down the beach,
leaving in her wake a running mob of scared Hawaiians.

On his final visit, Vancouver asked about the health of the
cows he had left the previous year. He was told the story of
the famous bull calf. It had been born when Kamehameha
happened to be at Hilo, on the other side of the Big Island.
The chiefs were so anxious to show him the calf that they
ordered it to be carried over the mountains on the backs of
native runners. The calf was fed on fish all the way, and in
three days arrived, healthy and kicking, to be admired by the
King.

Vancouver also brought goats and geese, and gave orange
and almond trees to the chiefs on various islands. He found
that the people were already growing delicious muskmelons
from seeds given to them by a British captain.

On his second trip, after enjoying a visit with Kamehameha
at his court, Vancouver went on to the island of Oahu and
made a strong complaint to King Kahekili. Vancouver's supply ship had anchored in May, 1792, off the mouth of Waimea
Stream on the northern shore of Oahu. The lieutenant in
command of the vessel had led a watering party up the stream
without being too watchful against possible attack. Accompanied by an astronomer from the ship and two sailors, he
had been trapped by a group of Hawaiians, and all were
killed except one of the sailors. Some muskets had been put

into their boat, and the natives may have been after these white man's weapons.

Vancouver was determined to have the guilty ones punished so that such a massacre would not happen again. Three natives who were blamed for the crime were brought to Vancouver's ship off Waikiki Beach and shot by a Hawaiian executioner.

The British captain tried to make peace among the warring chiefs in the Islands. Time and again he scolded the white traders for selling firearms and powder to the natives. Sometimes the guns were old and dangerous. One of the doctors with Vancouver saved the life of a young chief at Kealakekua Bay whose right arm had been shattered when a worthless gun exploded. But despite this good advice from his friend Vancouver, Kamehameha kept on buying guns and powder. For him the wars were not yet over.

Vancouver gave Kamehameha a British flag to fly in front of his house, and promised to send him a sailing ship with the compliments of His Majesty King George. Just before he left, Vancouver received from Kamehameha a paper which, the captain believed, made it clear that the King was putting his country under the protection of Great Britain. This pact was not legal, but it is true that in the early years the British people had more influence with Kamehameha than the few Americans who were to be found in Hawaii.

Soon after Vancouver's ships sailed beyond the horizon, old King Kahekili, who now ruled all the islands except Hawaii, died at Waikiki. He left his dominions divided between his younger brother Kaeo and his son Kalanikupule. They soon disagreed and started a conflict that was to be the end of them both.

Kaeo and his warriors in 1794 decided to make a sneak attack on his nephew Kalanikupule. For several weeks they fought around the southwestern part of the island of Oahu.

It looked as if young Kalanikupule would be defeated. In his trouble he got the idea of enlisting the help of some of the foreigners on three ships anchored near Honolulu.

One was an American ship, the *Lady Washington,* under Captain John Kendrick. The other two, the *Jackall* and the *Prince Lee Boo,* were under the command of an Englishman, Captain William Brown, who a year or two before had been the first foreigner to enter the harbor of Honolulu. Captain Brown was willing to sell firearms to Kalanikupule. He also agreed to let George Lamport, the mate of the *Jackall,* and eight other sailors act as volunteers in the battle soon to come.

The white men were stationed in boats along the eastern arm of the body of water nowadays called Pearl Harbor. Their fire on the flank of the invaders helped to bring victory. Kaeo, who was a prime target in his cloak of yellow feathers, was killed and his men fled.

Captain Brown decided to celebrate the victory by firing a salute from his ship. By mistake, one of his cannons was loaded with grapeshot. The salute crashed through the side of the *Lady Washington,* anchored nearby. The blast killed Captain Kendrick and several of his officers who were having dinner with him.

Under another captain, the *Lady Washington* soon sailed away for China. Brown's two ships remained in Honolulu Harbor for several weeks, butchering and salting down the four hundred hogs paid him for his help in the war.

King Kalanikupule decided that, if he could capture these two fine ships, he might be able to use them to overcome Kamehameha. On New Year's Day, 1795, he and his warriors took the *Jackall* and the *Prince Lee Boo* by surprise. The two captains were killed, and the members of the crew, who were ashore, were made prisoners.

The sailors were forced to fit out the ships to sail against

Kamahameha. Off Waikiki on January 12 the King and Queen, with their chiefs and warriors, came aboard. But Mate Lamport had a plan. At midnight he led a desperate uprising. The Hawaiians on board were killed or driven off. The royal family were put ashore in a canoe. Then the two ships sailed for China, glad to get away from the dangers of helping Hawaiians in their civil wars.

Kamehameha at this time was ready to start his final campaign to take over all the islands. He had built up a well-trained army of no fewer than sixteen thousand men—the largest army that had ever been seen in the Islands—and a fleet of big canoes to transport them across the rough waters between the islands. Sixteen white men were by now serving him. John Young and Isaac Davis were once more in charge of the cannons.

First Maui and then Molokai were captured by his warriors. Then Kamehameha crossed over to Oahu. The canoe fleet stretched from Diamond Head along Waikiki Beach. Then the warriors poured ashore and began skirmishing against the defenders among the grass huts of the little village of Honolulu.

Battling every bit of the way, the army of Kalanikupule was slowly driven up the steep valley behind Honolulu. Spears flew, and clubs crashed down on helmeted skulls. John Young's cannons belched fire and iron.

The retreat turned into a rout. At the top of the pass, the fleeing defenders found at their backs the thousand-foot precipice called the Pali. Some of the fleeing warriors escaped on one side or the other, over the knife-edged ridges. A few managed to scramble down the cliff trail leading to the north side of the island. But many of the retreating soldiers were forced to jump to destruction over the horrible cliff. Only a

few lived to tell the story of the relentless tactics of the conquering Kamehameha.

In this decisive battle of 1795, Kalanikupule was forever
overthrown. He wandered in the mountains for several
months but was finally captured and sacrificed to Kamehameha's war-god. Except for the leeward islands of Kauai
and Niihau, all the Hawaiian chain was under the sway of
Kamehameha.

The King now began to build up his forces to invade
Kauai. His foreign carpenters set to work to construct a
forty-ton ship, but it was not finished when in April, 1796,
he decided to make the ninety-mile trip across the channel.
Instead of the ship, he used a fleet of canoes.

To keep the people of Oahu from rising at his back, he
took the strong measure of killing all the hogs on the island
and destroying other foodstuffs. A famine resulted. And before his fleet was halfway to Kauai, a heavy storm arose and
many canoes were turned over. When he put back to Oahu,
mourning for his drowned warriors, he heard that another
revolt had broken out on the Big Island. Kamehameha went
with his fleet to Hilo, where his men hunted down the rebels
and sacrificed their leader.

Learning that the capture of Kauai would not be easy,
Kamehameha spent several years building up a fleet of hundreds of double canoes, with long, deep hulls joined by a
platform and driven by foreign-type sails. He also had his
men build some small schooners, and stored up six hundred
muskets, fourteen small cannon, and forty swivel guns.

Early in 1804 he was once again prepared to launch an
attack from Oahu against Kauai. But once again trouble held
him back. This time it was a plague which struck down many
of his best chiefs and men. Kamehameha himself caught the

disease and for a while it seemed that he would not survive. He had to postpone the conquest of Kauai.

Thereafter, Kamehameha gave his islands the first peaceful rule they had enjoyed for many, many years. He turned his efforts to giving a wise leadership to the new kingdom he had founded, and which he was to guide for the next fifteen years.

What kind of person was King Kamehameha, who is often called "the Napoleon of the Pacific"?

A story was told by a Scotch sailor, Archibald Campbell, who had been well treated by Kamehameha and was leaving to go back to England. The King of the Sandwich Islands asked Campbell to give his compliments to King George of Britain. "I told him," Campbell said, "that, though born in his dominions, I had never seen King George; and that, even in the city where he lived, there were thousands who had never seen him. He expressed much surprise at this, and asked if he did not go about among his people, to learn their wants, as he did? I answered that he did not do it himself, but that he had men who did it for him. Kamehameha shook his head at this, and said that other people could never do it as well as he could himself."

Kamehameha did indeed give his personal attention to the needs of his people as well as to those of his foreign friends. He had a strong mind that enabled him to govern, and he firmly put down disorder and crime. He could be ruthless in war, but when the fighting was over, he could forgive and act like a statesman.

He was faithful to the traditions of his race and his religion. Yet he was curious about the new things that foreigners had brought to his realm, and adopted any new ideas that seemed sensible to him. Perhaps his strongest trait was his ability to arouse the devotion of his followers. He was foremost among all the Hawaiian chiefs of his time in learning from the white men, and took many of them into his service. But they were his advisers only, never his masters. He was always a king.

One of Captain Cook's lieutenants had described Kamehameha in 1789 as having "as savage looking a face as I ever saw; it however by no means seemed an emblem of his disposition, which was good-natured and humorous, though his manner showed somewhat of an overbearing spirit." An American seaman described him in 1803 as "a perfect savage, but evidently destined by nature, both physically and mentally, to be a chief." Another in 1809 put him down as "a man of very good natural abilities, of tender feelings, and aiming to be just, making a very good ruler."

Perhaps the best description of the King in the middle of his reign was given by Campbell: "In 1809 the king seemed about fifty years of age; he is a stout, well-made man, rather darker in complexion than the natives usually are, and wants two of his front teeth. [About twenty years before, Kamehameha had knocked out his own teeth as a sign of mourning for a friend.] The expression of his countenance is agreeable, and he is mild and affable in his manners, and possesses great warmth of feeling; for I have seen him shed tears upon the departure of those to whom he was attached, and has the art of attaching others to himself. Although a conqueror, he is extremely popular among his subjects; and not without reason, for since he attained the supreme power, they have enjoyed repose and prosperity."

Kamehameha led his people in practicing the arts of peace. After the civil wars were over in 1795, the land was untilled and many were starving. The King urged his people to raise food, and he himself could be seen working up to his middle in the mud of a taro field. He told his people at such times that they would not need to show the usual high respect for his royal person by falling on their faces in reverence to him every time he passed by, with his digging stick in hand. His subjects said of him: "He is a farmer, a fisherman, a maker of cloth, a provider for the needy, a father to the homeless."

Kamehameha was the first of his people to learn to ride horseback. The first horses in the kingdom were brought into Kona in 1803. Thus was fulfilled the words of an early prophet: "White people shall come here; they shall bring dogs with very long ears, and men shall ride upon them." The King was the first of the line of fine Hawaiian riders, both men and women, who loved nothing better than to race bareback along the beach or gallop down dusty trails. A parade of *pa-u* riders—lovely girls in trailing skirts astride prancing steeds—is still a feature of the Kamehameha Day celebrations in memory of Hawaii's first king.

The King could look very imposing in any costume, whether it might be one of his priceless cloaks of thousands of yellow feathers, or else the full uniform of an officer of the British Navy. His favorite informal garb was a roomy Chinese dressing gown which had originally been a gift to King Kalaniopuu from Captain Cook. When ceremonies were over, though, Kamehameha liked to slip into a malo, or loincloth, and relax with his friends, or else go out surfboard riding.

Being a Hawaiian ruler was not an easy task. During the *makahiki* festival, he had to prove his skill at self-defense. He had to stand while other chiefs threw three spears at him. He had to catch the first in his hand, and with it ward off the other two. The spears were thrown in deadly earnest, and if they had killed the King, nobody would have been punished.

But Kamehameha was equal to the contest. No less a person than Captain Vancouver swore that once he saw Kamehameha ward off six spears hurled at him at almost the same moment. Three he caught in the air with one hand. Two more he broke by parrying them with his own spear. The sixth he dodged, so that it fell harmlessly.

Kamehameha followed his old pagan religion to the end. "These are our gods, which I worship," he told a visiting Russian captain in 1816. "Whether I do right or wrong in thus worshipping them, I know not, but I follow my religion, which cannot be bad, since it teaches me to do no wrong."

And he believed in his gods. One of the large craters on the top of Mount Hualalai on the Kona coast of Hawaii erupted in 1801. The lava poured down, flattening stone walls, trees, and houses before it. It covered several villages, destroyed plantations and fishponds, and filled up a deep bay along the coast. The priests tried to appease the anger of the gods by offering many sacrifices. Numerous hogs were thrown alive into the burning stream of lava, but all to no avail.

Then one day Kamehameha went to the volcanic river. He cut off part of his hair and threw it into the molten streams. A day or two later the lava ceased to flow. Kamehameha's people believed that he had saved them from the anger of the volcano gods.

The Melting Pot Simmers

WHY IS HAWAII OFTEN CALLED "THE MELTING POT OF THE Pacific"? Because for generations it has been a place where people of many nations and races have mingled their blood to form a harmonious new race, with a rich background of customs and ideas.

Even before the arrival of Vancouver, foreigners had been welcomed by the Hawaiians. It was the fashion for every chief to have at least one white man as an adviser. Kamehameha had the ability to win the loyalty of foreigners and to keep them in his service for years, or even a lifetime.

At least eleven men from other lands were living on the island of Hawaii in 1794—not only Americans and Englishmen, but also Irish, Portuguese, Genoese, and Chinese. A quarter of a century later, between one and two hundred foreigners lived there. Hardly a ship touched the Islands without leaving a deserter or two behind to enjoy their tropical charms. Escaped convicts from Australia were not unknown. Some of the strangers were vagabonds or wretches who lived in rags, without homes or regular meals.

Many of the white men, though, became solid citizens. The King found jobs for them to do. A white man automatically ranked as a chief, but he could not own any land or build a house that would be his forever. Some of the Europeans who settled in the kingdom married Hawaiian girls. Several families prominent in the history of Hawaii began in the days of Kamehameha.

John Palmer Parker, for instance, came from Massachusetts. He was put in charge of the cattle herds that had descended from Vancouver's cows. George McClay, another Yankee, had been a ship's carpenter. This good-natured, honest fellow built some twenty small sailing ships to add to Kamehameha's fleet.

An American Negro named Anthony Allen, who had been a slave back in Schenectady, New York, arrived in 1810 and soon became one of the most respected citizens of Honolulu. On his farm on the plain toward Waikiki he supported his Hawaiian wife and three children by selling milk from his cows and goats and by running a sort of sailor's boarding-house.

George Beckley, like John Young and Isaac Davis, was British. A sea captain, he commanded Kamehameha's fort in Honolulu. Another British tar, Alexander Adams, was captain of the King's most valuable ship. John Harbottle, who had been mate of the *Jackall* of London, became the chief pilot for Honolulu Harbor, which had been surveyed in 1796 by a British sloop of war.

Archibald Campbell, the Scot mentioned earlier, had lost

both feet from frostbite in Alaska. He was taken care of by Kamehameha and set up in business as a cloth weaver. He found no fewer than sixty white men living on Oahu when he arrived there in 1809. Another Scot was the King's doctor. Another, William Stevenson, had escaped from the convict settlements of Australia. He was noted for having been the first man to distill a fiery liquor from the root of the ti plant. He soon reformed, though, and restricted his drinking to New Year's Day. The rest of the year Stevenson labored from dawn to dark, raising European vegetables in his garden.

An Englishman named John Howel, who arrived as a clerk on the *Lady Washington*, decided to settle in Hawaii. He tried several times to convert King Kamehameha to the Church of England. The King finally told him: "You say that your God will shield those who truly believe in Him. Give me proof of this by jumping off the cliffs above Kealakekua Bay. If you are unharmed, then I will embrace your religion." After one look at the jagged precipice, Howel decided that the life of a missionary was not for him.

Another Englishman, James Beattie, had been an actor on the London stage. The earliest plays given in the Islands were put on by Beattie for Kamehameha, who was very fond of entertainment. The scenery was made of sheets of kapa, or native cloth of beaten bark. These were cut up, pasted together, and painted to look like a castle or a forest.

A European play, with words written by Beattie, was once seen by Archibald Campbell. "The part of Malvina was performed by the wife of Isaac Davis," he reported. "As her knowledge of the English language was very limited, extending only to the words 'yes' and 'no,' her speeches were confined to these monosyllables. She, however, acted her part with great applause.

"The audience did not seem to understand the play well,

but were greatly delighted with the after-piece, representing a naval engagement. The ships were armed with bamboo cannon, and each of them fired a broadside, by means of a train of thread dipped in saltpeter, which communicated with each gun, after which one of the vessels blew up. Unfortunately, the explosion set fire to the forest, and nearly consumed the theater."

One of the earliest foreign residents of Honolulu was a Spaniard. His name was Don Francisco de Paula Marín, but the Hawaiians called him "Manini." He served as Kamehameha's interpreter, as his business manager, and sometimes as his tailor. Manini was a born gardener and brought into the Islands dozens of useful plants. He knew something about medicine and attended Kamehameha on his deathbed.

As a boy, Manini had gone from southern Spain to California on an exploring expedition. He was still very young when, in San Francisco, he delivered a load of fruits and vegetables on board a ship that was about to leave that port in 1791. The lad fell asleep, and when he awoke he was on his way to the Sandwich Islands.

He went ashore and wandered from one place to another until he met Kamehameha, and thereafter followed the fortunes of the King. Manini lived in Honolulu until he died, more than forty-five years after his arrival. He had more than thirty children, and some of their descendants still live in Honolulu today.

Most of the early plants brought into the Islands came from seeds, roots, or cuttings imported by Manini through friends of his in other parts of the world. Early in his experiments he grew pineapples, oranges, grapes, peaches, melons, figs, lemons, beans, cabbages, potatoes, horseradish, carrots, asparagus, corn, lettuce, roses, and tobacco. None of these, of course, were native to the Hawaiian Islands. Later he grew coffee, cotton, clover, tomatoes, turnips, peppers, wheat, and barley. He went in for making coconut oil, castor oil, soap, sugar, molasses, pickles, and lemon syrup. He also tried his hand at manufacturing lime, tiles, hay, nails, cigars, candles, beer, wine, and brandy. But other people thought he was stingy since he never gave seeds or slips for them to plant in their gardens.

Manini's house in town was a two-story adobe building, with a large garden running up the Nuuanu Stream. He got butter and cheese from his dairy herd. He also owned an island in Pearl Harbor, on which he raised hogs, goats, and rabbits.

Some of the foreigners thought that Manini, who had been baptized a Catholic, was too ready to swallow pagan beliefs. Manini found it safer to take part in Hawaiian celebrations such as the *makahiki*. But he visited many Hawaiians as a doctor and, as he confided to one Catholic visitor, he secretly baptized more than three hundred natives before they died, hoping to save their souls if not their bodies.

Kamehameha not only invited foreigners to work for him, but also was interested in trading with the ships that came to his domain, and soon became a skilled bargainer.

One day he played a little game with a Yankee trader, who had offered him twenty quarts of rum in exchange for some hogs. The King stood by while the man ladled out the amount in a quart measure. When the count was finished, Kamehameha objected that there were only nineteen. Sure that he had counted right, the Yankee offered to do it again. "Never mind —let's split the difference," the King suggested. The trader refused and started to measure the rum a second time. Kamehameha chuckled and said he would take the man's word for it. The King was not trying to cheat. He was merely having some fun pretending to haggle in the manner of the Yankees.

Throughout his reign Kamehameha swapped his products for foreign goods, and built up a treasure in dollars and in various articles from overseas. Because of its fine harbor, Honolulu soon became the foremost seaport in the eastern Pacific —a distinction it still holds. It was such a busy place that in 1804 Kamehameha moved his court there from the Big Island.

The King had still not given up his dream of conquering the two islands to the northwest. He had sent several envoys to Kauai to demand the submission of the ruler there, but so far had not been successful. But in 1810 an American sea captain offered to bring the King of Kauai to Honolulu, leaving the first mate of the ship as a hostage for good treatment.

The King of Kauai was in his early twenties. His name was Kaumualii, which means "Oven of the Nobility." He was a nephew of old Kahekili and a son of Kaeo, who had been killed at Pearl Harbor. Kaumualii was a handsome fellow who looked more English than Hawaiian. He was one of the best swimmers in the Islands, which was saying a great deal, since Hawaiians have always been famed for water sports. Kaumualii had picked up some English and was a great admirer of King George of England; in fact, he had adopted the name of George for himself in true Polynesian fashion.

Kaumualii had been shrewd enough to obtain some American friends, who were building a ship for him. These tactics were so clever that Kamehameha decided to give up the idea of taking Kauai by invasion. Instead, he had invited the young King to sail to Oahu.

Off Honolulu, Kamehameha came aboard, and on deck made a pact by which Kauai would become a tributary kingdom. Kaumualii would continue on the throne until his death, but thereafter Kauai and Niihau would become part of the Kamehameha domain. After Kaumualii had taken a look at Kamehameha's fleet, he decided to agree. Thirty small sloops and schooners were drawn up on the shore at Waikiki, and about a dozen more were moored in the harbor of Honolulu.

Kaumualii went ashore to take part in a feast of friendship. Some of Kamehameha's advisers decided that the best thing to do would be to poison the young King of Kauai. But when Kamehameha heard of the plot, he rejected the idea fiercely, saying, "This is not a time of open war, when a prince can be slain like a robber!"

The young King might have been killed, nonetheless, had he not been warned by Isaac Davis, the Welshman. Quickly Kaumualii hurried home to Kauai. Soon afterward Davis, loyal adviser of the first King of the united Islands, himself died of poison, victim of the plotters' grudge.

During this same year, at least a dozen ships visited Honolulu. Two of them were British, two were Russian. The rest were American. The Yankees were indeed moving into the Pacific. The first celebration of the Fourth of July in Hawaii of which there is any record was held aboard the *New Hazard* in 1811. The following year, Kamehameha himself spent the Fourth of July aboard an American ship, where he was given three cannon salutes and took part, as reported, in a "grand feast."

The supply ships for the Oregon post of the American trader John Jacob Astor always stopped at Hawaii. On the first of his ships to reach Honolulu, the *Tonquin*, twelve Hawaiians were taken aboard as sailors. They were all massacred, along with the rest of the crew, by Indians off Vancouver Island on the northwest coast of America in the summer of 1811. But nothing could keep the sea-loving Hawaiian lads from shipping on foreign vessels to see the world and make a little money.

The War of 1812, between England and America, reached even into the far Pacific. A British vessel captured by the Americans entered Honolulu Harbor in May, 1814—the first war vessel flying the United States flag ever to do so.

The distinctive Hawaiian flag, which today is the flag of the State of Hawaii, goes back to the War of 1812. Ever since Vancouver had given him a British flag, those colors had flown outside Kamehameha's residence. But during the War of 1812, an American remarked that he should be more neutral.

The King thereupon designed a flag of his own, which combined features from both the British and the United States flags. It kept the Union Jack in the upper quarter, but the rest of the field was spangled with alternate stripes of white, red, and blue, "like those of the American flag, in allusion probably to the number of islands" rather than to the thirteen original states.

The Hawaiian flag was first flown in foreign waters in 1817 when Kamehameha's trading brig arrived off China. The baffled harbor master had never seen colors like these before. But the flag has now been flown for almost a century and a half, over Hawaiian cities as well as Hawaiian ships.

Sandalwooders, Pirates, and Russians

KING KAMEHAMEHA DECIDED TO GET RICH. HE LOOKED AROUND for a product he could sell to foreigners that would bring him a fortune.

It was all well and good to peddle to visiting ships a supply of fresh fruits and vegetables, but even though pork was a royal monopoly, the provision business did not bring in much cash. The King took over the oyster beds of Pearl Harbor and hired divers to bring up pearls and shells, but this trade soon petered out.

Once the King thought he could run a diamond mine. Some ignorant sailors climbed an old volcano crater near the Waikiki shore and found some gleaming crystals. But these turned out to be worthless, and the only result was that thereafter the hill was called Diamond Head.

Nobody suspected that the best source of ready money in Hawaii at this time was an ordinary-looking tree that grew up in the hills. Its wood was so fragrant that it brought high prices in China. There it was used for making idols and sacred objects, for fancy boxes and carvings, for incense sticks, and for burning on funeral pyres. The oil was used in medicines, perfumes, and cosmetics. It was called sandalwood.

The first man to take a load of Hawaiian sandalwood to China was probably the vengeful Simon Metcalfe, the captain whose son was thrown off the *Fair American* to drown. But the wood was of such a poor grade that the Chinese did not buy it, and for many years this treasure in Kamehameha's back yard was overlooked.

The story of sandalwood as a commercial jackpot began on New Year's Day, 1812, when three American traders picked up a shipment of logs while on their way to China with a cargo of furs. When they came back they were able to pay King Kamehameha a good price for the sale of the wood. In return he gave them a contract allowing them a ten-year monopoly on the trade. After the War of 1812 there was a boom in the sandalwood business, which for some years was the main source of money for Kamehameha and the ruling chiefs who followed him.

The King ran the business himself. He conserved the supply by putting a tabu on the cutting of young trees. He not only heaped up money in his treasury as a result of selling the wood, but added a number of ships to the royal fleet, all of them paid for with sandalwood.

One ship, for instance, was bought for twice its volume in fragrant logs. A pit was dug in the ground the same size as the hull of the ship. The hole was twice filled with sandalwood brought down from the hills by toiling Hawaiians in the

King's service. That is the way the value of a sailing ship was measured in the early days.

The sandalwood era was marked by the arrival in the Islands of a hardened gang of pirates. In the spring of 1818 a mysterious ship appeared off the Big Island. Its captain, who called himself Turner, said that she was the *Santa Rosa* from the Argentine region of South America, whose people were revolting against Spanish rule. He offered the ship to Kamehameha for four hundred tons of sandalwood. This was a bargain rate, considering that the *Santa Rosa* was an American-built vessel, armed with eighteen cannons and carrying a cargo of dry goods. The crew settled ashore and seemed to have plenty of money. Some of them owned gold and silver ornaments of the sort usually found in Catholic churches.

Three of the crew came to Honolulu, and one day one of them was heard making strange boasts in a tavern. He was taken before the governor of Oahu, and the true story then came out. When the ship had reached the Pacific, a master's mate named McDonald had led a mutiny and assumed the name of the real captain, Turner, who was put ashore in Chile with thirteen men who refused to join the mutiny. The pirate ship then attacked other vessels and raided towns on the South American coast, now and then robbing and burning a church.

One day, when Griffiths, the first lieutenant of the pirate ship, had been sent with forty men to cut off some ships in one port, their faithless fellows in the *Santa Rosa* sailed off to Hawaii and left them. But Griffiths, in a captured brig, sailed after them. He and his forty thieves settled ashore in the Islands. McDonald, fearing their vengeance, somehow seized the brig and sailed away from Hawaiian waters.

He was wise, for another Argentine warship was on the pirates' track. In September this vessel, a forty-four-gun frigate named the *Argentina*, reached Hawaii. The crew was so sickly that out of 260 men, there were hardly enough healthy ones to do the ship's work. The captain of these avengers, a dashing young Frenchman named Hipolito Bouchard, demanded that Kamehameha give back the *Santa Rosa* and turn the pirates over to him for punishment.

The King agreed. Captain Bouchard pardoned most of the rascals and added them to the crews of his two ships, which then sailed for Honolulu to refit. Then they went on to the island of Kauai to round up more of the mutineers. Four of these were handed over by King Kaumualii, but the ringleader Griffiths was not among them.

Captain Bouchard swore that unless Griffiths were delivered to him, he would bombard the village of Waimea with his cannons. Three days later Griffiths was arrested, court-martialed, and shot on the beach by four marines.

Bouchard's two ships then departed, after enlisting eighty Hawaiians to add to their motley crews. The Argentine "patriots," as they called themselves, began raiding the helpless Spanish settlements of California. One of their acts was to burn the little town of Monterey. They acted, in truth, much more like pirates than like patriots. The people of Hawaii were glad to be rid of them.

Other visitors to Kamehameha's kingdom included Russians. During his reign some of them tried to take over the Islands, and for a whole year the Russian Czar's flag flew over parts of Kamehameha's realm. Had the Russians succeeded in their aims, Hawaii, instead of being an American state today, might be a Soviet base off America's western shores.

Early in the last century Russia, seeking good spots for new colonies, sent out several round-the-world expeditions. The first of these, made up of two ships, scouted through the Hawaiian chain in 1804.

One of these ships came back in 1809, sailing down from Alaska, the Russian headquarters in the Pacific. Its captain probably had secret orders to see if he could start a Russian settlement in these important islands. Off Honolulu, Kamehameha came aboard and asked whether this was an English or American ship. When told that it was Russian, he said: "*Maikai*—good." He was then presented with "a handsome scarlet cloak, edged and ornamented with ermine." Kamehameha tried it on and gave it to his men to be taken ashore, but he never wore it again. This sample of Russian generosity probably did not impress a monarch who owned several priceless cloaks, each made of thousands of rare feathers.

The Russian ship returned to Alaska to report that the time was not yet ripe to grab the Sandwich Islands, but that Kamehameha and Kaumualii were not very friendly with each other. Perhaps the Russians could get their way by stirring up trouble between the two kings.

For the next few years the Russians turned their colonizing efforts toward building up Fort Ross in California. But when that failed, they once more thought of getting a foothold in Hawaii.

The Russians sent a trading ship to Hawaii. On the last night of January, 1815, it was wrecked in a bad storm off Waimea, Kauai. The Hawaiians saved much of the cargo of valuable furs, but the ship was a total loss.

The Russian governor of Alaska thought that the need to recover this cargo would give him a fine excuse to set up a base in the Islands. As his secret agent he decided to send a crafty young German soldier of fortune named Dr. George Anton Scheffer.

The doctor had been working for Russia for several years, and happened to be in Alaska. He arrived on the Big Island on an American trading ship. He got into Kamehameha's good graces by curing him of a feverish cold, and in return was given a piece of land on Oahu.

Posing as a man of science, Scheffer traveled around the Islands and was amazed at their richness. He began raising various crops, such as tobacco. While waiting for the arrival of Russian ships and settlers, he went to Kauai and got on very good terms with King Kaumualii.

Kaumualii was still afraid that Kamehameha would try to take his islands away from him, and at first was glad to have the help of the two shiploads of Russians that landed at Waimea. Scheffer got him to sign a paper by which Kaumualii put himself under the protection of the Czar. Kaumualii then raised over his house a flag showing the double-headed Russian eagle.

Scheffer got busy entrenching himself on the island of Kauai. Kaumualii gave him a lovely valley and four hundred Hawaiian workers to turn it into plantations. The Russians built several strong forts, where Scheffer mounted his cannons and flew the Czar's flag.

He also started to build a fort over on the water front of Honolulu. But John Young, who was still Kamehameha's most trusted adviser, did not like the thought of having a Russian fort dominating Honolulu Harbor. He sent all the Russians away.

However, John Young thought that having a fort there was not a bad idea, and he had his own workmen finish the building. He set sixty cannons on top of an eighteen-foot wall. Inside were barracks for Kamehameha's soldiers. At night the guards sang out every ten minutes, in English, "All is well!"

All was not well on the island of Kauai. Scheffer had gotten the King to give him all the sandalwood trees growing on that island. The King also promised to give the Russian Czar one half of Oahu in return for the aid of Scheffer's army in capturing the island. It looked as if the era of civil wars was not yet over in the Sandwich Isles.

Meanwhile, a quite different sort of Russian visitor was meeting with King Kamehameha at Kealakekua Bay on the Big Island, far to the southeast. This was Captain Otto von Kotzebue.

Kotzebue had visited Hawaii a dozen years before, on the first Russian round-the-world cruise. Now he was in command of the little brig *Rurik*, on a similar mission. Even before the *Rurik* dropped anchor off Kamehameha's headquarters, Kotzebue heard wild tales about the acts of Scheffer. The pilot who came out to guide Kotzebue to an anchorage was so frightened when he heard that the ship was Russian that he tried to jump overboard. On shore, Kamehameha had lined up four thousand soldiers to keep the strangers from landing.

But Kotzebue soon explained that his master the Czar did not wish to conquer the Hawaiian Islands and would punish any of his subjects who acted unlawfully. He and his men spent a pleasant day ashore as guests of Kamehameha, who presented Kotzebue with a splendid feather cloak to take back as a present to the Czar.

When the *Rurik* went on to Honolulu, the people there were even more frightened. Kotzebue decided to make a survey of the harbor, and as markers his men used long poles with flags on top. The villagers almost started a riot. They remembered that Scheffer had once flown a Russian flag on a pole and said the words, "I take possession of this island." They thought Kotzebue was trying to do the same thing. He solved the problem by replacing the poles with long brooms.

Kotzebue sailed away to the north, to seek the Northwest Passage that Cook had failed to find. Before the *Rurik* returned to Hawaii in the fall of 1817, Scheffer's attempt to take over the Islands had come to a head.

Kamehameha had warned young King Kaumualii that the Russians should be sent away at once. Kaumualii himself began to tire of his bad bargain. The Russians in Alaska feared that Scheffer's behavior would cause trouble with other nations.

The American traders living in the Islands, however, had most to do with the downfall of the Russians on Kauai. They did not like the idea of having the Russians get a corner on the sandalwood trade. The Americans were few in number, but they persuaded King Kaumualii to tell the Russians to get in their ships and go back to Alaska.

The Americans won out. The revolution succeeded without bloodshed. Dr. Scheffer paddled in a canoe to one of his ships, leaving behind the cargo of furs, the rich lands he had been given, and tons of precious sandalwood. He was lucky to escape across the channel to Honolulu. His ship was leaky, and took five days to make the trip, with the crew pumping all the way.

At Honolulu, John Young refused to let the troublesome doctor come ashore. Scheffer went to China, and from there to Russia, to plead his case before the Czar himself. But his wild attempt was disowned, and thereafter the Russian flag was never again to fly over any part of the Hawaiian Islands.

The last commander of a Russian warship to meet King Kamehameha was Captain V. M. Golovnin, who stopped at Hawaii on his way to Alaska. "Kamehameha is already very old," he wrote; "he considers himself to be seventy-nine years of age. . . . However, he is alert, strong, and active; he is temperate and sober; he never takes strong drinks and eats very moderately. In him one sees a most amazing mixture of childish deeds and of ripe judgment and actions, that would not disgrace even a European ruler."

Golovnin took back to Russia a young Hawaiian named Laurie who had hidden away on his ship. The lad was taught to speak Russian and liked St. Petersburg for a while. But he hated three things: ice, snow, and beards. Clearly, Russia was no place for Laurie, and he was sent back to Hawaii a year later.

Captain Golovnin was something of a prophet when he set down these words: "Were it possible to introduce the Christian faith and the art of writing among the Sandwich Islanders, they would in one century reach a state of civilization unparalleled in history. . . . If a few well-educated, patient people, capable of observing things carefully, like the missionaries of old, should settle in the Sandwich Islands, there is no doubt that they would soon become famous."

About a year later, the first shipload of Christian missionaries sent to Hawaii sailed over the horizon.

The Landing of the Longnecks

A DARK-SKINNED YOUTH SAT WEEPING ON THE STEPS OF YALE College in New England. "Why?" asked students who paused at his side.

"Because I am ashamed of my ignorance. Who will help me learn about the world and about the words of Christ?"

The students pressed him further. They found that the lad's name was Henry Opukahaia. He had been born in Hawaii around 1792. His parents had died in the civil wars, and he had been brought up by an uncle who was a pagan priest at the heiau at Kealakekua Bay where Cook had been worshipped as a god.

But the boy had been unhappy and had run away to sea. He had sailed to New England with a kindly American captain and now lived with that sailor's family there.

66

The students were touched by Henry's story and offered to be his teachers. They found him an eager pupil. Henry was not only reverent and hard-working. He also had a sense of fun that expressed itself in doing imitations of people he knew. He would ask, "Who dis?" and then comically take off someone's behavior.

Obookiah, as he was called, became a famous person in New England. He was sent to a special school that had been started to train American Indians, Pacific natives, and others to become interpreters for missionaries who might be sent out. Henry became a good Christian, started to translate the Bible into Hawaiian, and dreamed of returning to his islands as a missionary.

It was not to be. Henry died of typhus fever at the mission school in 1818. But in his death he did more for his religion, perhaps, than if he had lived to sail back to his native land. The sermon given at his funeral by a noted preacher was widely printed. A little book about him spread the wave of interest even further. The story of the lad who wept in heathen darkness was the beginning of the first Christian mission ever sent to Hawaii.

This group was sent out by an association of New England churches, the American Board of Commissioners for Foreign Missions. The work of this board was to become as impressive as its long name.

The "First Company," as it came to be called, gathered on the Long Wharf at Boston on October 23, 1819. They sang a hymn, "When Shall We All Meet Again?" and then were rowed out to the brig *Thaddeus*, to begin a five-month voyage around Cape Horn to the Sandwich Islands.

The seven families who formed the First Company are still remembered in Hawaii. The leaders were the Reverend Hiram Bingham and the Reverend Asa Thurston. Both these men

were from New England colleges. But the group also included
a farmer, his wife, and their five children. Another man was
a schoolmaster, and another a mechanic. Another important
person was a printer, Elisha Loomis, who had loaded his press
and cases of type on board. Another was a doctor, who nowadays would be called a medical missionary. All the men were
married; the board thought it would be best if they took wives
and families along. Mrs. Thurston had been married less than
two weeks before sailing.

Also aboard the *Thaddeus* were four young Hawaiians,
who had been gathered together in New England and trained
at the mission school. Their portraits had been painted by
Samuel F. B. Morse, who later was to invent the telegraph,
and a picture of them was sold to raise money for the work
of the mission.

One of the four "missionary boys" was named George P.
(for "Prince") Kaumualii. He was the son, by a commoner,
of King Kaumualii, the ruler of Kauai. At the age of seven
the boy had aroused the dislike of Kaumualii's Queen, and
his father had paid an American sea captain to take him to
Massachusetts and give him a good education. When the money
ran out, young George enlisted in the United States Navy.
He served in the War of 1812, cruising against the pirates of
Algiers and getting wounded in a ship-to-ship battle.

George wound up at the mission school in Connecticut,
where he not only studied English but relearned his native
Hawaiian tongue. The missionaries hoped that George would
be a good interpreter and that his father would be so glad to
see him return that the King would be especially friendly to
the New Englanders who brought the boy back home to
Kauai.

On the morning of March 30, 1820—two hundred years
after the Pilgrims stepped ashore at Plymouth to bring Chris-

tianity to New England—the pilgrims on the *Thaddeus* sighted the snow-capped summit of volcanic Mauna Kea, Hawaii's tallest mountain. The people of the First Company stood at the rail to get their first glimpse of the islands to which they were bringing the Gospel. Would they be greeted with open arms? Or would they suffer the fate that befell Captain Cook?

The *Thaddeus* rounded the northern point of Kohala and skirted the barren coast. Through spyglasses the missionaries could see their future converts, moving about on shore. But no canoes came out to the ship. What was happening?

The four Hawaiian lads were excited over being near their islands again. Two of them could wait no longer. They piled into a boat with the ship's supercargo and headed for the beach. But they returned three hours later without having touched land. Some fishermen offshore had given them news too good to keep.

Old King Kamehameha had died almost a year before. He had been true to the last to the grim war-god that he had served so well. But on one point he had changed his mind. When he was near his end, according to old custom a new temple was built. For it a human sacrifice was demanded. But the old King refused the priests, saying, "The men are tabu for the King." He meant that his son Liholiho would need all the living men he could find to uphold the throne in the dangerous days that would come.

Amid cries of mourning from a hundred thousand throats, "The Lonely One" passed into a greater loneliness. His bones were concealed in a secret cave by one faithful comrade. "Only the stars of the heavens," runs the saying, "know the resting place of Kamehameha."

Liholiho, his twenty-three-year-old son, was proclaimed ruler of the Islands under the title of Kamehameha II. He was an amiable young man, but his will was not always strong.

However, he had the advice of several older chiefs, both men and women. Together the King and his Privy Council took a bold step. They decided to overthrow the old nature worship that the foreigners in the realm had often called "pagan idolatry."

The ugly carved images that frowned above the heiau were to be defied and cast down. Most risky act of all, a strong tabu would be broken.

This ancient thou-shalt-not forbade men and women to eat together. No woman in ancient Hawaii had been allowed to eat pork, bananas, coconuts, or certain fish. Only three years before, a woman had been executed by Kamehameha I for breaking such a tabu. Liholiho's mother and stepmother were both on the Privy Council. They all decided to take part in an act that would be an open defiance of their gods. The act was called *ai noa,* or "free eating."

Liholiho ordered a public feast to be held at Kona. At this table, for the first time in Hawaiian history, women openly ate beside their menfolk. The heavens did not fall. When the meal was over, the young King commanded that all the old temples be broken down and all the grim idols hacked to bits.

Some people clung to the old religion. They rallied around Liholiho's cousin, to whom had fallen the honor of protecting Kamehameha's old war-god Ku. A battle was fought between his supporters and those of the King. But the defender of Ku was killed, along with his faithful wife, who, following the old custom, fought by his side. Thereafter the idols were worshipped only in secret.

All this was wonderful news to the people arriving on the *Thaddeus.* The old pagan gods had been cast off, but the Hawaiians had no other beliefs to take their place. Even the old high priest had come to doubt the power of Ku and Kane. The missionaries could not have come at a better time. They brought the Gospel to a nation that was looking for a new truth.

Off the coast, the Prime Minister of Hawaii came aboard the *Thaddeus*. He was a big, jolly Hawaiian who had been nicknamed Billy Pitt. He wore a white dimity jacket, black silk vest, nankeen pantaloons, white cotton stockings, a plaid necktie, and a top hat. Several lady chiefs were with him, swathed in many folds of kapa cloth. Billy Pitt offered to ride down the coast on the ship to the village of Kailua, where Liholiho had his court. Only the King could give permission for the missionaries to land in Hawaii and begin preaching the new religion.

At Kailua on April 4, the missionaries and the King had their first meeting. Liholiho was dining with his five wives at his house near the shore. He was glad to accept a gift of a fine spyglass, but was in no hurry to allow the Americans to stay in his domains.

He thought it over for four days. Perhaps his English and French friends would object to giving people of another nation so much power over the minds of the Hawaiians. But old John Young swayed the balance. He thought that Christian ideas were badly needed in the realm of Kamehameha II.

Liholiho agreed that the newcomers might land at Kailua, but they could stay only one year, on trial. Four days more of discussion were required before he gave permission for some of the missionaries to go to Oahu and settle in the town of Honolulu.

The *Thaddeus* company then scattered. The Thurstons were chosen by ballot to stay at Kailua along with the doctor and his wife and two of the "missionary boys." The others voyaged to Honolulu to set up the first Christian church there.

The town of Honolulu was vastly different from the neat New England villages that the missionaries had left behind.

It sprawled along the harbor's edge, dotted with adobe store-houses, shops, and one tavern after another. The rest of the settlement was "a mass of brown huts, looking precisely like so many haystacks in the country; not one white cottage, no church spire, not a garden or a tree to be seen save the grove of coconuts."

Up the dusty street walked the First Company. The wives were the first white women that most of the Hawaiians had ever seen. The burly natives ran along beside them, peering beneath the sunbonnets and shouting to each other: "The faces of these women are small and set far back, and they have long necks!"

Thereafter the missionaries were called "the Longnecks." And everything they did was closely watched by a staring crowd of Hawaiians. Day and night, the natives peered through the windows of the houses and wondered aloud why these strange people had come to Honolulu. Could they be a war party? "No," said others, "they have brought their children with them. A war party would have left the little ones behind."

There was much to be done in Missionary Row. The dirt-floored houses, with roofs thatched with grass, had to be made into homes, with the help of gifts of furnishings from friendly Honolulu storekeepers. In such a house was born on July 16, 1820, the first white child to see the light in the Sandwich Islands. He was Levi S. Loomis, son of the printer.

A frame house shipped from Boston in pieces arrived on December 25—a very welcome Christmas gift for the missionaries. It was set up with great rejoicing. Those who visit Honolulu can still walk through that house, for it has been kept as a museum.

The Reverend Hiram Bingham and his friends at once started church meetings. Sunday became a different kind of day in Honolulu. Chiefs and their ladies came to listen to sermons and to call on the Longnecks. The wives from New England were much in demand to sew clothing for the Hawaiian women of high degree, who wanted gowns in the latest fashion. Precious yards of cambric were sewn into huge dresses, looking like enormous nightgowns. The chiefs demanded shirts and suits. The King put in an order for a dozen ruffled shirts and a broadcloth coat.

The main thing that was achieved by the missionary women, though, was setting up the first schools in the Hawaiian Islands. On May 23 the first small school was opened. A woman named Pulunu brought her two small children. Pulunu learned to write a whole sentence on her slate. It said: "I cannot see God, but God can see me." She held it up for the little ones to admire.

Of course many of the first pupils were children. But the oddest part of the work was that during the early years, most of the students were grownups.

And most of them belonged to the class of chiefs. The ruling group said quite frankly: "If this new word is good, we wish to possess it first ourselves. If it is bad, we do not want to let our people know the evil of it." Thus many of the first classes were held to instruct the royal family and their supporters. Boki, the governor of Oahu, and his pretty wife Liliha learned to read and even to pray. By the end of the first year, mission schools had been opened in several towns in the Islands. They had about a hundred pupils of both sexes and all ages, but mainly grownups.

Two of the missionaries had soon gone from Honolulu to the island of Kauai. King Kaumualii was delighted to see his long-lost son George again. They rubbed noses affectionately, and George was made second only to the King himself on Kauai. The grateful ruler rewarded the captain of the *Thaddeus* with the gift of $1,000 worth of sandalwood. And he asked the missionaries how to become a good Christian. He loved to listen to the Bible stories all day long, even when he was in swimming.

The missionaries who had been left at Kailua on the Big Island also got on well there. King Liholiho heard their sermons with respect, and for a while even tried to learn to spell in English. The First Company had made themselves a needed part of Island life. At the end of the year of trial, Liholiho granted them permission to stay as long as they desired.

Liholiho and the Missionaries

King Kamehameha II, also known as Liholiho, had not forgotten that King Kaumualii of Kauai had promised he would pay tribute to the Kamehamehas.

One July day in 1821, Liholiho suddenly decided to go to Kauai and get a personal renewal of that pledge. He got into a small open boat with Governor Boki and thirty other people and set out to sail to Kauai.

He had never before been to that island, and did not know whether he would be received with open arms or with pistols. His followers were terrified as they plunged across a hundred miles of stormy channel. They had no food or water. When they said they had no compass, Liholiho merely pointed with his finger to show the direction to be taken.

The boat was twice nearly capsized, but Liholiho said: "Bail out the water and sail on. If you return with the boat, I will jump overboard and swim to Kauai!"

The young King got to Kauai in spite of his foolhardiness. There he was greeted loyally by Kaumualii, who repeated his promise to leave Kauai at his death to Liholiho. But Liholiho had his own ship come to Kauai to meet him. At the end of his visit, poor Kaumualii was lured aboard and taken back to Honolulu as a royal prisoner. To make sure that he would not get home to Kauai, he had to marry the widow of Kamehameha I, the strong-minded ruler called Kaahumanu, or "Feather Cloak."

The next trip that Liholiho planned was to prove fatal. Remembering his father's pact with Captain Vancouver, the young King considered that the Sandwich Islands were under the protection of Great Britain, a country he much admired. He had been given a six-gun schooner by the British government, fulfilling Vancouver's promise to send a ship. And in the fall of 1823, Liholiho decided to visit England and talk to his fellow ruler, King George.

Liholiho, his wife Kamamalu, and Governor Boki and his wife, with various other courtiers, left for England in November, 1823, on a passing whaleship. They did not arrive in London until the following May.

They settled in a fancy hotel suite, purchased European dress of the latest fashion, and looked forward to being entertained by royalty. Soon, however, they were hit by a disease which, despite the doctors, quickly brought death. It was the measles. The King and Queen could not fight against these foreign germs. She died on July 8, 1824, and the King, full of grief, lasted only until the fourteenth.

Before leaving Honolulu, Liholiho had named his nine-year-old brother as the heir to the throne. This meant that the kingdom was really run by Kaahumanu as regent. She was beautiful in Hawaiian eyes, for she was six feet tall and weighed over three hundred pounds. Her husband Kaumualii had died just a few weeks before Liholiho died in far England. In Kaumualii's will he left Kauai and Niihau to the Kamehameha family. Now, in truth, all the islands of the chain were united under one crown.

George P. Kaumualii, the "missionary boy" who had been brought home on the *Thaddeus*, had not fulfilled the hopes of the Reverend Hiram Bingham and his band. George had forgotten about his good training and had begun to act again like a veteran of the sea wars of 1812. When he heard that his father had died in Honolulu and that he had been disinherited, he told Bingham that he feared the King had been poisoned, and wondered if he, George, would be next.

George started a civil war. One Sunday morning in August he led a group of discontented Kauai chiefs against the old Russian fort at Waimea, which was held only by a handful of Kaahumanu's soldiers. But the attack failed bloodily. George hid in the hills with his wife Betty, a daughter of his father's friend Isaac Davis. Their child was born during the brief war, and for the rest of her life bore a Hawaiian name meaning "Rebel Girl." Two years later, like his father a prisoner of Queen Kaahumanu, George P. Kaumualii died in Honolulu, last of the royal sons of Kauai.

Right from the first, the missionaries had been busy in the kingdom of the Kamehamehas. The first Christian church in the Islands was dedicated on September 15, 1821, in Honolulu, on the site of the present Kawaiahao Church, which has been called "the Westminster Abbey of Hawaii." The first Christian marriage in the Islands united one of the "missionary boys," Thomas Hopu, with a Hawaiian girl from the island of Maui. The first chiefs to have a Christian wedding were married in October, 1823.

The number of missionaries in the Islands had been increased with the arrival of the Second Company on the ship *Thames* in April, 1823. By the following year, mission stations were running on Kauai, at the port of Lahaina on Maui, and at Kailua and Hilo on the Big Island.

As yet few Hawaiians had earned the privilege of being baptized into full church membership. The mother of Liholiho was baptized only an hour before her death in 1823. Thereafter this rite was given to no one for almost two years. Then a famous blind Hawaiian man was taken into the Lahaina congregation.

Although Queen Kaahumanu had taken a lead in overthrowing the idols, she had been at first rather offhand in her attitude toward the missionary band. She would sometimes call upon them right after swimming in the ocean, and drip sea water on the floor of their sitting room. Slowly the Queen Regent became less proud and haughty. She would sometimes drop her game of cards and try to puzzle out the letters in the spelling book. Then, around 1824, she began pushing the conversion of all her people. Often she would come to listen to the preaching on Sunday, riding in a little American-built wagon pulled by six strong Hawaiian men.

Another lady chief took a strong stand in defending the Christian faith from the perils of paganism. Her name was Kapiolani. She got the idea of helping out the work of the mission at Hilo by defying the Hawaiian fire-goddess, Pele, at the edge of the bubbling fire pit that was the dwelling place of this powerful deity.

Kapiolani led a hundred-mile march from Kona to the smoky volcanic crater of Kilauea, on the slope of the vast mountain dome of Mauna Loa. Hawaiian priestesses who dwelt here among the spouting fountains of melted rock tried to change the mind of this chieftainess. One of them tried to dissuade Kapiolani by waving a piece of kapa which was supposed to be a *palapala*, or sacred scroll of Pele. "I too have a *palapala*," Kapiolani answered, waving a hymnbook.

At the edge of the fiery pit, Kapiolani broke an old custom. The visitor was supposed to tear off a branch of berry-bearing ohelo, throw half of it into the crater, and say: "Pele, I offer some ohelos to you, some I also eat." Kapiolani broke the branch but ate all the berries, refusing to share with the goddess. Then she made her famous challenge, in a voice that could be heard above the roaring of the flames: "Jehovah is my God. I fear not Pele!"

A prayer was uttered, and all the party then slowly marched back without being overwhelmed with fire by the enraged goddess. Kapiolani spent Christmas at the Hilo mission, and scholars flocked to study there.

Two things made it especially easy for the Hawaiian people to become good Christians. One was that this religion satisfied their feelings. They loved to talk and sing. Hundreds of people from all over the region would flock on Sunday, by canoe and on foot, to hear the preaching, and to take part in the hymn singing. Again, the idea of tabu had been one of the main points of their old beliefs, and the Ten Commandments were quickly received by the Hawaiians as simply a new variety of *kapu*.

Sunday became a day of rest. Nobody held sports competitions on the beach, no children splashed in the surf, no travelers went to and fro on their business. Sunday horseback riding, in particular, was frowned upon by the chiefs. The little churches were filled not only by natives but by some townspeople and visiting ship captains, who were surprised to be able to attend a Congregationalist service so far from Boston.

The missionaries were also successful in fighting against

liquor drinking, smoking, and stealing. Even the old dances and sports and songs were considered to be heathenish. Some visitors felt that the gay old life of ancient Hawaii had been smothered by a grim Puritanism. But even the "blue laws" ordered by the chiefs could not wipe out the happy frolicking of the easygoing Hawaiians.

The second great appeal of the missionaries was their knowledge of reading and writing. Along with religion, they brought education. The Hawaiians were most grateful for being taught to know the world through books.

The schools were very popular. The missionaries learned to speak Hawaiian as soon as they could, and most of the teaching was carried on in that language. The schools of Honolulu could be heard a long way off, for the pupils recited their lessons aloud in chorus. Like most peoples without written traditions, they had wonderfully good memories, and loved to learn many chapters of the Bible by heart.

One of the missionary wives remarked that "they teach each other, making use of banana leaves, smooth stones, and the wet sand on the sea beach for tablets. Some read equally well with the book upside down or sidewise, as four or five of them learn from the same book with one teacher, crowding around him as closely as possible."

The school idea spread as bright students were given schoolrooms of their own in other parts of the islands. Six years after the coming of the *Thaddeus*, no fewer than four hundred Hawaiians had become teachers, and the students numbered twenty-five thousand. Four years later, more than a thousand schools were scattered among the villages. By 1832, more than half of all the adult Hawaiians had learned to read.

All this time, remember, the students were mainly grownups. The children had to wait. Their parents did not want them to gain this new knowledge until their elders had done so. Not until 1832 was the first group of child pupils rounded up, clothed, washed, and set to work at their slates.

The Hawaiians before Cook, of course, never knew how to write. Kamehameha II asked a missionary to write out his name on a paper. Looking at the letters spelling "Liholiho," the King said: "It looks neither like myself nor any other man."

There is a story that one missionary sent a present of seven melons to another, with a note that mentioned this number. The Hawaiian messenger delivered only six. Asked where the missing one was, he complained: "How could you know there were seven? The other melons could not tell you, for I hid from them when I ate the seventh!"

The newcomers could not spread their learning until an alphabet for writing Hawaiian had been invented. This the missionaries did. To the five vowels were given the usual European sounds. To these were added seven consonants—*h, k, l, m, n, p,* and *w.* These twelve letters enabled any Hawaiian word to be written down.

Then the printing press of Elisha Loomis was unpacked and put to work. Elisha was only twenty when he arrived in Hawaii, and his press was probably older than he was. But it had to do. He set up shop in a grass-roofed house in Honolulu, and on January 7, 1822, he ran off the first sheet ever printed in the North Pacific region. It was part of an eight-page spelling book in Hawaiian. A few weeks later, King Liholiho visited the shop and ran off a page with his royal hands.

Now that something to read was available, the number of scholars rose quickly. Soon Loomis had to move to a bigger shop, with walls of coral blocks (the building can be visited today on King Street in Honolulu). Here, with Hawaiian helpers whom he had taught, he began to print many books.

At first there was trouble in the shop because the Hawaiian

language needed many hundreds of extra pieces of type with the letters *k* and *a*, yet it did not need most of the letters of the English alphabet. But by the summer of 1827, Elisha received enough type from the United States to enable him to set up fifty-six pages in Hawaiian at a time.

One of his first books was a sixty-page collection of the Hawaiian words of hymns. The most popular early publication, though, was *Ka Pi-a-pa*, an eight-page leaflet that was reprinted eight times. It showed the alphabet, numerals, punctuation marks, lists of words, verses of Scripture, and a few short poems. It was like the hornbook used in New England in early times, and was the main reading matter in half the schools for ten years.

The missionaries began very soon to translate the Bible into Hawaiian. But it was a giant task. Over a period of almost twenty years the Scriptures were issued piecemeal as they were translated and printed. The Hawaiians eagerly devoured each section as it came from the groaning press. In 1826 no fewer than eighteen thousand copies of the Sermon on the Mount were distributed, and in the next year twenty-five thousand were needed.

For printed matter the Hawaiians were willing to trade taro, potatoes, cabbages, bananas, coconuts, sugar cane, eggs, firewood, fish, and even their canoe paddles. If they had nothing to barter, the missionaries would give them books anyway.

The first edition of the complete New Testament came out in 1832, but the complete Bible was not ready until 1839. Various other editions have come out since that time. The Bible in the Hawaiian language is still in print and is still in demand.

The presses rolled merrily. In the first eight years, the Honolulu shop ran off four hundred thousand copies of twenty-eight different books and tracts. When the Lahainaluna School was started on the island of Maui in 1831, a printing house was opened there. At first the students learning to set up type had to make their own composing sticks. The first book printed at Lahainaluna was a translation of a book called *Scripture Geography*.

This little school press also had the honor of putting out in 1834 the first periodical ever issued in the North Pacific region. It was a little four-page weekly paper in Hawaiian, illustrated by woodcuts. It was called *Ka Lama Hawaii*, or "The Hawaiian Luminary." Two years later, the *Sandwich Island Gazette*, the first newspaper in the region, and the first printed in English west of the Rocky Mountains, came out in Honolulu.

Among the most useful books were English-Hawaiian dictionaries to help the people of Hawaii to learn the tongue of the English and American people, who were now the main foreign influence in Hawaii. But in the early days, the mission presses turned out at least sixty different books or pamphlets. These included not only the Bible and sermons, but also legal studies, a translation of *Pilgrim's Progress*, and textbooks in geography, mathematics, astronomy, natural history, and even anatomy.

The power of the press in making Christianity at home in the Islands was immense. One of the missionary wives was able to claim proudly that the proportion of those in Hawaii who could read and write was "greater than in any other country in the world, except Scotland and New England."

Kamehameha III
and Foreign Gunboats

THE REIGN OF THE THIRD KAMEHAMEHA WAS THE LONGEST IN all of Hawaiian history. It was marked by many striking events and problems. One of the chief problems was this: How would the Hawaiians be able to get along with the growing number of foreign people coming to their Islands?

Liholiho's younger brother Kauikeauoli, which means "Suspended in the Blue Sky," became King Kamehameha III in 1825, when he was only eleven years old. Naturally, he ruled through a regent, who was the missionaries' friend Kaahumanu. But when she died in 1832, the young King angrily disregarded his other advisers and plunged into a wild life for a while.

After two years, he decided that he should be a better example to his subjects, and began to wonder how he could best bring law to his lawless kingdom. In 1835 he proclaimed a code that would punish murder, theft, fraud, and drunkenness, and that would apply not only to Hawaiians but to foreigners. After that Kamehameha III began to give more and more thought to making his monarchy into a constitutional kingdom where everybody could expect justice.

Sometimes the foreigners made his task easier, sometimes harder. The foreign nations most strongly represented in Hawaii were America, England, and France.

The Americans were not only missionaries, who worked for the good of the natives, but also traders, who sometimes wanted merely to make money.

Sandalwood had been, since the days of Kamehameha I, the main source of income. During the four years from 1817 to 1821, American traders handled cargoes of sandalwood worth about $400,000 when sold in China. The heirs of old Kamehameha I and the chiefs of the kingdom who shared in the income from sandalwood went on a buying spree. A secondhand yacht called *Cleopatra's Barge* was bought by them for $90,000. Grass shacks were stuffed with fine silks, foreign suits and dresses and hats, cut-glass bowls and porcelain dishes, and imported furniture. Fancy carriages and even billiard tables were in demand. One chief paid $800 just for a wall mirror, and another paid $10,000 for a brass cannon that he fancied.

At this time in Hawaii, "wooden money" was used. There were few coins for exchange, and a load of sandalwood became the usual measure of value. The chiefs decided that their people should pay their taxes in sandalwood. Thus the natives had to go into the wet and windy mountains and chop down their share of trees.

At first this work appealed to the Hawaiians as a kind of game. Sometimes they would go collecting wood at night, by torchlight, and sing as they dragged the logs down to the shore. But it was not always fun. The trees became scarcer and the seekers had to go further to find the wood. Men and women tied six-foot logs to their backs and climbed to and fro between the mountains and the measuring pits, both by day and by night. Often they had nothing to eat but moss or wild roots. They spent most of their time collecting wood and had no chance to grow taro and other food crops. The hard labor in wet forests did much to injure the health of the Hawaiians and cut down the number of them left.

The common people got nothing for the wood they gathered, and the chiefs seldom bought anything that they really needed. The greedy traders, who made huge profits, would get the chiefs to order various rich toys and when they could not pay, would offer them credit. But even before the sandalwood was nearly all gone, around 1830, the traders—most of them Americans—began to ask the United States government to send a warship to Hawaii to force the chiefs to pay their bills.

By 1824 the chiefs owed the traders about $300,000. Two years later, a visiting American ship of war got the Hawaiian government to promise to pay the money. This was the beginning of the national debt. But the claims caused much trouble and were not finally settled until 1843—long after the sandalwood boom had collapsed.

The English influence in the Islands continued to be strong. It was reinforced when on May 6, 1825, the bodies of Kamehameha II and his wife, who had died of the measles in London, were brought back in state on the British warship *Blonde*.

This ship was commanded by Lord Byron, a cousin of the famous poet and a friendly man whom the Hawaiians at once admired. He met with the chiefs and told them that from now on they would have to make their own laws and carry them out without the help of the British Navy or any other foreign force. Lord Byron gave them some good advice—trial by jury was started in Hawaii as one result—and then sailed off to let them try to learn how to be real leaders of their people. England continued for years to have many friends in Hawaii.

The French were few in the Islands, but early in the reign of Kamehameha III the French government decided to try to get Hawaii under its control. A ship put ashore some French settlers and three Catholic priests and three lay brothers. Queen Kaahumanu told the captain of the ship to take them all away again, but he refused. Although they did not have permission to settle, the group stayed. The first Mass was held on July 14, 1827. The first person to be baptized was a child of Manini the Spaniard. The Frenchmen got the King to give them some land in Honolulu, and on it, in January, 1828, the first Catholic chapel was opened in the Islands.

At first the New Englanders did not worry about the newcomers. They felt that the Hawaiians would never want to become Catholic. But as time went on and a number of the natives became converted, the Protestants asked the chiefs to send away the priests. Almost all the chiefs were willing to do this, for they felt that by now the Gospel brought to them in the *Thaddeus* should be the official religion of Hawaii. Any of their subjects who were willful enough to become Catholics were disloyal and should be punished. And during the next ten years quite a few Hawaiians had to work on a road gang because they dared to change their religious beliefs.

Governor Boki of Oahu, who had returned from England with Lord Byron on the *Blonde*, felt he was a rival of Kaahumanu. Since she favored the American missionaries, Boki decided to favor the French missionaries. But in 1828 the help of Boki was lost to the Catholics.

Boki (there is a story that he took the name of a dog named Bossie) wanted to get rich by trading with the white men and by driving his many followers to work hauling sandalwood for months at a time. One day a ship from Australia brought word that somewhere in the South Pacific there was an island covered with sandalwood trees that would bring someone a fortune. Chief Boki fitted out two ships, poured into them five hundred of his loyal retainers, and set sail for the Fiji Islands.

One of these ships limped back to Honolulu eight months later with a tragic story to tell. They had found the treasure island, but disease and battles with the Fiji people had wiped out many of the crew. The other ship, which had separated from the first, was never heard of again. This flagship of Boki's was probably blown up by accident. The crew usually kept bags of gunpowder strewn on the lower deck, where they often sat and smoked carelessly. Thus, through an explosion Boki and his party were removed from the Honolulu scene.

The rest of the chiefs in April, 1831, ordered that the Catholic priests be sent away. When months passed and the priests still remained, the chiefs fitted out one of their sailing ships and sent the priests off to Mexican California. But four years later a priest came to look over the land and see if a second attempt to set up a mission should be made.

As a result, youthful Father Arsenius Walsh arrived in Honolulu. He was a British subject, and the French who sent him thought that he would be allowed to stay on that account. He was ordered to leave, but the captain of a visiting French warship got permission for Walsh to stay, provided he did not try to baptize any Hawaiians. A few of the natives were baptized anyway during the next four years.

Two of the first group of priests returned from California in April, 1837. They were ordered to go back on the same ship that brought them. A fine international mix-up resulted. The ship was owned by a Frenchman, but sailed under the British flag, and during the passage from California had been chartered to an American merchant. Arguments were fiery and endless. The two priests stayed on board for several months, until the captains of two visiting ships—one English, one French—decided that the priests should leave at the first chance.

One of the priests did sail at the end of October, but a few days later, two more priests sent by the bishop in the South Pacific came to Honolulu. These were Columba Murphy, a jolly Irishman who had visited Hawaii before, and L. D. Maigret. These newcomers were at once forbidden to land, but the fact that Murphy had recently been ordained was not revealed, and when the British consul stated that he was not a priest, Murphy was permitted to go ashore. Father Maigret bought a schooner and departed with the remaining priest who had been awaiting a ship.

The French government considered itself the protector of all Catholic priests in the Pacific. This and other facts persuaded Kamehameha III in June, 1839, to proclaim what amounted to an edict of religious toleration, which stated that Catholics would no longer be punished for their beliefs. Just a month later, though, another French warship arrived with orders from Paris to use force, if necessary, to make the chiefs of Hawaii beware of incurring "the wrath of France."

Captain C. P. T. Laplace was making a round-the-world cruise to promote French commerce. He accused the Hawaiians of breaking a treaty made with a French captain. He leveled his cannons at the houses of Honolulu and demanded that the chiefs sign a new treaty. It provided that Catholicism should be allowed, that land be given for a Catholic church, that the French flag be saluted with twenty-one guns, and

that the Hawaiians deposit $20,000 in cash with him as a
guarantee of good behavior.

Laplace prepared to land his soldiers and level his guns
against the Hawaiians and the American missionary families.
The King was staying on the island of Maui and could not
be reached. It seemed that war was surely coming. But the
governor of Oahu agreed to all the demands of Laplace. There
was nothing else to do. Raising the cash was difficult, but the
shopkeepers of Honolulu managed to find $20,000 among
them. (Seven years later, a French admiral gave back the
money; the coins were still packed in the original boxes.)

The King came to Honolulu as soon as he could. But by
the time he arrived, Captain Laplace had thought up some
more demands. Two of these were especially disliked. One
would give to any Frenchman accused of a crime in the Islands
the right to be tried before a jury of foreigners named by the
French consul. The other would give trade preferences to
French goods, especially wine and brandy, even though a law
prohibiting the sale of liquor to Hawaiians had been passed
the previous year.

Kamehameha III could not do anything else but sign these
demands. The Catholics were thus free to carry on their work
in his kingdom. Their mission was on a firm footing by the
time the Bishop of Eastern Oceania visited it in May, 1840,
along with three other priests—one of them the expelled Father
Maigret. A Catholic church of stone was begun, and schools
were opened on other islands. By the end of the year, more
than two thousand people had been baptized on Oahu alone.
The first Catholic printing press was set up the following year,
to publish tracts and texts in Hawaiian.

Nevertheless, the French government kept on bothering the
Hawaiians, and it seemed to many people that it was looking
for an excuse to take over the Islands, as France was doing in

other parts of the Pacific. A French admiral seized the Marquesas Islands in July, 1842, and from there sent a sloop of war to Hawaii, bearing orders which made further demands on Kamehameha III. These would have given the Catholics a commanding position in the Islands and allowed the priests to name certain officials of the Hawaiian government.

This time the King stood firm. He could not yield another inch without giving up his right to lead the Hawaiian people. He was trying to gain recognition of Hawaiian independence by treating with various governments, including that of France. He refused to sign any more disgraceful pacts, and the sloop sailed away empty-handed.

The time of "gunboat diplomacy" had not, however, passed away. The British consuls in Honolulu had been troublesome, hoping to get a chance to have the Islands annexed by England. On February 10, 1843, the frigate *Carysfort* arrived in Honolulu Harbor to protect British interests. It was commanded by a young man named Lord George Paulet. Without listening to anyone except Alexander Simpson, the British consul, Lord George ordered that the King must at once recognize the consul formally, or else the guns of the *Carysfort* would bombard Honolulu.

Before the eight-hour limit was up, the King agreed. But this was only the beginning of a series of demands, which included a payment of more than $100,000. It was clear that Lord George intended to force Hawaii under British rule. The King gave in under protest, hoping that Lord George's superiors would redress the wrong.

The Hawaiian flag was hauled down on February 25, and British soldiers marched into the fort to the strains of "God Save the Queen." Lord George took over three of the King's ships. On one of these sailed Simpson, the British consul, on his way to London with a report on the annexation of Hawaii.

On the same ship was a young American named James F. B. Marshall. Unknown to the British, Marshall was the official envoy who would present the Hawaiian side of the story in London. He carried secret documents which had been drafted by Dr. Gerrit P. Judd, the King's main adviser, in the privacy of the royal tombs, using the coffin of Queen Kaahumanu as a writing desk. The reports that these rival messengers, Simpson and Marshall, were carrying wound up on the same desk in the British Foreign Office.

The British flag flew over the Islands for five months. Lord George did not get along well with anyone, and soon began to meddle in the home affairs of the Hawaiian government. A body of troops was formed, to be called the "Queen's Regiment" but to be paid from the King's treasury. The prohibition laws were loosened. Things got so bad that on May 11, after several protests, Dr. Judd resigned. To prevent the seizure of the public records, he hid them away in the same royal tomb where he had written protests to London.

Growing resistance to British rule was strengthened by the arrival of the American commodore, Lawrence Kearney, in his flagship. An open break with Lord George was prevented by the arrival of Rear Admiral Richard Thomas, commander of the British squadron in the Pacific, on his ship *Dublin*.

Admiral Thomas decided to restore Hawaiian independence at once. On the morning of July 31, a great crowd gathered on King Street. On horseback, Kamehameha III was given a salute of twenty-one guns from the warships in the harbor, to recognize his kingship again.

The King and his chiefs then went to the Kawaiahao Church for a thanksgiving service. During his speech, the King uttered the words which ever since have been the motto of Hawaii and today form the motto of the State. They are:

Ua mau ke ea o ka aina i ka pono ("The life of the land is preserved in righteousness").

The site of the restoration ceremony was named Thomas Square in honor of the admiral, who came ashore for the next six months, during which time his merry personality won the heart of everyone.

Exactly four months after the restoration of the kingdom, the hard work of Kamehameha III and his advisers in trying to get international recognition of Hawaiian independence bore fruit. In London a declaration was signed in which the independence of the little Pacific kingdom was recognized by the Queen of Great Britain and by the King of France. The United States had been given the chance to sign this paper as well, but had declined for fear of "entangling alliances." However, in the summer of 1844 the American Secretary of State reaffirmed American recognition of Hawaiian independence.

Still the foreign troubles of Kamehameha III were not over. In 1849 the French consul in Honolulu was still trying to get France to take over the Islands. At his request a squadron of two French war vessels arrived, and Rear Admiral Legoarant de Tromelin sent ten demands to Kamehameha III. These ranged from equality of worship to reduction of duty on French brandy and the punishment of naughty schoolboys who had put their hands in holy water.

To enforce these demands, De Tromelin landed a French force to take over various government buildings. The soldiers spiked all the guns in the fort, poured the gunpowder into the sea, and smashed furniture and clocks in the governor's house. The King's yacht and some foreign vessels were seized. Ten days later De Tromelin sailed away, having forcibly protected the interests of the French subjects in the Islands. There were only twelve of them.

Again a mission was sent to Europe to ask for justice. It was headed by Dr. Judd, who took with him the King's nephews, two princes who were both later to rule Hawaii. No new treaty with France was gained, but the young brothers, who saw not only Europe but the United States on their return journey, gained a useful view of the world that was to influence their ideas when they came to the throne.

The final attempt of France to overawe the island kingdom came soon after Dr. Judd's return. A warship arrived early in 1851 and repeated the infamous ten demands of De Tromelin. The King protected himself in a clever way. He signed a secret proclamation that would place Hawaii under the protection of the United States should the French try to seize the Islands. Then the American ship in the harbor would fire on the French ship, if necessary.

When this news reached the French captain, he changed his tone at once. He cut down his demands, signed a temporary agreement, and sailed off to France. Thus, after many years, the hovering shadow of French annexation was lifted.

Relations with Great Britain and America also improved over the years. The need to be friendly with the United States, the country closest in distance to Hawaii, was underlined when, in the middle of 1848, the news came to Honolulu that gold had been discovered in California.

The march of the American people to the Pacific Coast made it seem to many thinkers that, as a part of "manifest destiny," Hawaii would be annexed by the United States after the admission of California. A special treaty was signed between the two countries in 1850. But in the fall of the following year, Kamehameha III still feared that shiploads of Americans might arrive from California and grab the Islands. Other Americans who had settled in Hawaii were shouting also for annexation.

To protect his people, the King had a treaty of annexation drawn up. Kamehameha III insisted, among other things, that Hawaii should be admitted to the Union as a state and not a territory. Final signing of the treaty was delayed for various reasons, and thus ended this rehearsal for the admission of Hawaii to the United States, an event that did not come about until more than a century later.

Lawmakers and Whale Hunters

THE LONG REIGN OF KAMEHAMEHA III WAS NOTED NOT ONLY for international clashes, but also for much progress inside the kingdom.

Honolulu became the business capital of the Pacific. Ships came there from Europe, eastern United States, Peru, Mexico, California, and China. Shoppers in Honolulu had their choice of hundreds of imported articles from all over the world. By this time the chiefs, made wiser by the loss of their sandal-wood income, would not buy expensive toys on credit. They had a very good idea of the value of an article. One store, however, was nicknamed "the big debt," because its goods were so tempting that families ran up large accounts there.

Trade was held back because there was very little money in use, and therefore barter of one article for another was common. A businessman in Hawaii in the past century had to be familiar with the values of no fewer than a hundred and fifty gold and silver coins, from all the trading nations of the world. The lack of small change was very bothersome. When an American exploring expedition came to Honolulu in 1840, the commander took his Spanish dollars and had them chopped with an ax into quarters and eighths to be used for change. The King allowed the first coining of money in 1846, based on the American scheme of dollars and cents. But American nickels and dimes were almost worthless until a law was passed in 1859 making them legal.

The chief advance during the reign was the change from a personal rule to a constitutional kingdom, in which the whim of one man was replaced by laws that were the same for everybody. This change did not come easily or speedily. But it was made easier because the chiefs believed that the missionaries who had come all the way from America to teach them religion could also teach them how to behave well in other ways.

Hiram Bingham, when he came to preach his first sermon in Hawaii in 1820, found a very good text in Isaiah, chapter 42, verse 4: He shall not fail nor be discouraged, till he have set judgment in the earth: *and the isles shall wait for his law.* The chiefs who learned the Commandments in the schools wondered how these rules could be made into the law of the isles.

During the rebellion of George Kaumualii on Kauai in 1824, some of the chiefs went to consult missionary William Richards about the right thing to do. After Queen Kaahumanu was converted, the chiefs asked the missionaries to write out laws that would be suitable. In 1829 the King proclaimed: "The laws of my country prohibit murder, theft, adultery, fornication, retailing ardent spirits at houses for selling spirits, amusements on the Sabbath day, gambling and betting on the Sabbath day and at all times."

The need for even stronger laws continued. William Richards was asked in 1838 to take an official position as adviser to the King and his Council, and he decided to do so. He resigned from the mission board and thereafter until he died he took a leading part in the government. Later other men of the Protestant mission held places in the kingdom, and succeeded in having many of their ideas written into the law of Hawaii.

The main problem of law in the Islands came from the fact that the rights of foreigners had never been clearly stated. Could these foreign residents own land or carry on a business? If they owned land, could they sell it to others? Some foreigners who did not understand the typical Hawaiian idea of landholding thought that their rights in Hawaii should be the same as the ones they were used to in their home countries. When they felt injured, they were likely to ask that an American or British or French warship be sent to protect their interests. The search for treaties was part of the answer. The other part required that the government of Hawaii should put its own house in order.

William Richards and the council of chiefs, to whom he had given lessons in the theory of government, began working on a written constitution for the people. The first result, which was called "the Hawaiian Magna Charta," was a declaration of rights and laws on June 7, 1839. The opening lines of this document, in which the King freely gave up many of his inherited powers, sound much like the opening of the American Declaration of Independence.

Christianity was written into the law of the land when the first Hawaiian constitution declared that nothing should be enacted which was "at variance with the word of the Lord

Jehovah." This was the Constitution of 1840, which brought to the Hawaiian people many new rights. Prominent among these was a body of elected lawmakers. Thus, for the first time, the common man in the kingdom had a share in politics. Another was the setting up of a Supreme Court to judge appeal cases. Other liberal ideas were found in this constitution. A dozen years later, the King liberalized the government even more in his Constitution of 1852.

Richards spent three years traveling in Europe, trying to get sound treaties recognizing Hawaiian independence. While he was gone, another American, a young lawyer named John Ricord, was helping Kamehameha III make other reforms. These were embodied in a series of "organic acts" written by Ricord in his spare time.

The first of these, passed in 1846, divided the executive branch of the government into five departments, each with a minister at the head who would be a member of the King's Privy Council. The third organic act, in 1848, improved the system of courts and judges. The first chief justice was another young American lawyer, William L. Lee.

Probably the most important was the second organic act, which went into operation in 1846. It swept away the outworn Hawaiian feudal system of landholding, and set up a new one which is still the basis for all the titles to land held in the Islands. This division of lands was called the Great Mahele.

This is the way the Mahele worked. First, all the land in the kingdom was divided between the King and his chiefs. This was accepted Hawaiian practice. Second, the King divided his land into two parts: "crown lands" which he kept for his own use and "government lands" which he turned over to the government. Many of the chiefs also surrendered some of their land to the government, and in return got a clear title to what they kept. Third, the government land was sold, not only to the common people, but to foreigners. This revolution in land-holding was complete when many of the traditional home-steads tilled by the commoners could be held outright by them under the law.

All these changes were recorded in the big Mahele Book. Everybody knew what land belonged to whom, and nobody had to fear that he would suddenly be thrown off the acres on which he worked and lived.

The New England missionaries helped on political matters, but their main work was, of course, still religious. They were shocked by many Hawaiian habits that still remained, and in their books and letters one can see the Polynesian scene through the eyes of proper Bostonians. One of them noted, for example: "I have seen a young chief, apparently not three years old, walking the streets of Honolulu as naked as when born, with the exception of a pair of green morocco shoes on his feet, followed by ten or twelve stout men, and as many boys, carrying umbrellas, and kahilis, and spit-boxes, and fans, and the various trappings of chieftainship. The young noble was evidently under no control but his own will, and enjoyed already the privileges of his birth in choosing his own path, and doing whatever he pleased."

About twenty years after the first arrival of the missionaries, a fresh wave of interest in religion swept the Islands. For various reasons, the Hawaiians began to think more seriously about their future in heaven. Whereas up to that time only about thirteen hundred had formally entered the church, in the two years 1838 to 1840 more than twenty thousand joined.

The "Great Revival," as it was called, brought to every mission station a line of Gospel-seekers who wished to be saved. The scenes there were like the camp meetings of the American back country. Each meeting brought out five or six thousand Hawaiians, who shouted and prayed aloud for salvation. Cripples led the blind to accept the Gospel. On one Sunday alone in 1838 the missionaries at Hilo baptized 1,705 converts and gave communion to 2,400 church members before sunset. Three years later, the church in that town numbered seven thousand people, making it the largest Protestant congregation in the world.

Despite various drawbacks, the success of the American missionaries in Hawaii was notable. By 1840 preachers who came from nearly every state in the Union could be found in every traveled part of the kingdom. In thirty-five years, no fewer than fifteen "companies" landed. They had many children. The new and vigorous blood brought into the Islands by these strong-minded Americans helped to change not only the complexion of the population, but often the course of Hawaii's future.

The job of converting the people was done so well that by 1863 the American Board back in Boston decided that Hawaii should no longer be considered a mission field. The churches in Hawaii were to serve as bases for the missionizing of other Pacific islands to the south.

The mission folk could thus go home if they liked. But at that time the United States was in the grip of a great civil war. The missionaries had spent their best years in the Islands, and wanted to remain there. Their children had grown up in Hawaii, were at home there, and did not want to go away. The young people could stay in the Islands, though, only if they could earn a living there. Most of them went into teaching, or business life, or agriculture, or government. The founding of many a new branch of work in Hawaii dates from the time when missionary families no longer received salaries from the American Board and had to think of a different sort of career.

One sad fact that faced the missionaries was the apparent

falling off of the Hawaiian population. All through the century the number of these people dropped steadily. The three hundred thousand natives found by Captain Cook declined by 1900 to fewer than forty thousand Hawaiians and part-Hawaiians.

Diseases brought in by foreign ships and people caused much of the decline. For instance, in 1848 an epidemic of measles came from Mexico and raged through all parts of the Islands, followed by whooping cough and flu. Ten thousand people died within a year. Five years later there was a smallpox attack that killed another twenty-five hundred people in eight months. A fifth of the Hawaiians in Honolulu were carried off by this scourge, which came back again in 1881. Another horrible disease was leprosy, brought in probably from China.

"Oh, what a dying people this is!" exclaimed one missionary in 1837. "They drop down on all sides of us and it seems that the nation must speedily become extinct." The missionaries gave as much medical help as they could, but few of them were doctors, and in their fight against disease they were opposed by poverty, filth, and superstition.

Other causes than disease were at the bottom of the decline in the Hawaiian numbers. For many years, about a fifth of the young men were away from the Islands, sailing about the globe instead of raising families. These offspring of the Polynesian voyagers made excellent sailors and were much in demand by sea captains. During three years at mid-century, about two thousand Hawaiians signed on foreign ships.

This was the great era of Pacific whaling, and Hawaii took a leading part in that great American industry.

The whaling trade for a good many years was the chief source of income for the people of Hawaii. In those days, the lamps of America were filled with whale oil, and the best candles were made from spermaceti. The oil was also used on machinery and in making soap and paints. Used for corsets and for umbrella ribs, the flexible whalebone, from the throat of the right whale, was at one time worth $5 a pound. Ambergris from whales was used to make perfumes.

The Pacific Ocean, for more than half a century, was the main hunting area of the whalers. Hawaii lay at the center of the most popular grounds, and had the only good harbors within a circle four thousand miles wide. It was natural for the whaleships to meet either in Honolulu or at Lahaina, Maui, to repair sails and stock up on their needs. Here they could buy fresh fruit and vegetables and beef. Here they could store their heaps of whalebone and casks of oil until a ship arrived to take the goods to the United States. Here the crews could rest and relax before going back to the dangerous game of finding the giant mammals and killing them on the open ocean with sharp lances.

The first whale was killed in Hawaiian waters in the same year that King Kamehameha I died. The two ships that discovered this hunting ground were Americans from Massachusetts. Soon after, another Yankee whaler discovered rich grounds off Japan. Other grounds lay in the South Pacific and in the north, to the Bering Sea and beyond. Hawaii was located about in the middle of these cruising areas.

Within three years after the first whale was killed at Kealakekua Bay, sixty whaleships had touched at the Islands. Thereafter, about a hundred a year used the ports there until 1840. Then there was a big jump to an average of four hundred a year for the next twenty years. In the banner year of 1846, almost six hundred ships touched Island ports. At such times, a man might clamber from one end of the harbor to the other over the decks of closely moored whaleships. The great mass of these were American; most of the remainder were British.

Each spring and fall, Honolulu was swamped by a wave of

whalemen ashore. Their captains were good customers for the hundreds of items, from anchors to needles, required by a sailing ship on a long voyage. They also bought food from the Hawaiian farmers and cattle from the drovers that herded their animals through the streets to the butcher shops. Other stock items were sugar, molasses, coffee, turkeys, hogs, and goats. The government did well through charging port fees and other taxes.

But things were not always rosy. The rough sailors kicked up their heels ashore and spent their liberty money in low taverns. Then, roaring, they would fight with native constables or break the many laws of the kingdom that strove for peace and order. One such outbreak in the fall of 1842, when about a hundred and fifty whaleships were in Honolulu Harbor, led to a bad riot when a whaleman was found dead in his jail cell. For several days the town was terrified by wild bands of sailors, who set fire to the police station and by accident almost burned up the whaling fleet, moored not far away.

More deserters than ever were to be found on the beach at Honolulu. Here a captain was likely to discharge any man that might cause trouble. Sometimes the shipowners desired to save money by having the men quit the ship without collecting all their pay. For several reasons, beachcombers, sick or disabled or just lazy, cluttered up the town. Sometimes the American or British consul would help such a man, but often he had nothing interesting to do and nowhere to go.

For such men, the mission people arranged the opening of a Seaman's Bethel in 1838, in charge of a pastor and his wife. They helped sailors to read and to study the Bible, and their services in the hall of the Bethel were so popular that a church was opened nearby to care for the spiritual needs of the foreign people in Honolulu.

Shipping on a whaler was the common way in which a Hawaiian lad might see the wide world. The life was hard, but often he could get ahead faster at sea than ashore, and most Hawaiians loved the forecastle life. Their fearlessness and courage became widely known. The prowess of one man is still remembered, as told by a missionary:

"Once in the icy waters of the Okhotsk Sea, a right whale was captured just at nightfall. A storm was brewing and the captain was anxious to have the body lashed to the ship before dark, but in the hurry an attempt to bend a hawser around the flukes of the whale repeatedly failed. A Hawaiian sailor seized the end of a line and, leaping into the icy waters, dove with it under the great monster, brought it up the other side and back to the ship. The hawser was quickly attached, and before it was too late the whale was made fast." Diving under whales in northern seas was all part of the day's work for a Hawaiian sailor.

The Last Two
Kamehamehas

Suppose you had been transported by a time machine back to the Hawaii of more than a century ago, at the end of the reign of Kamehameha III. What sights would you have seen?

Honolulu was then a growing city. The downtown area spread up from the busy water front, where beside the docks rose a flour mill, a machine shop, a warehouse, and a three-story customhouse. There also lay a shipyard and the walls of the old fort, which was used mainly as a prison.

Near the tower of the Bethel Church was a barnlike central market where gathered people of all classes, jostling each other in friendly fashion and haggling for meat, poultry, and fresh vegetables. Through the street, carriers lugged their burdens on poles with loads dangling at either end. Now and then a neat carriage rolled by, but most of the traffic was made up of saddle horses, hand-drawn carts, and a few creaking ox wains.

Pride of the downtown area was a new courthouse, which had been built of coral blocks cut from the reef by prisoners. For the next twenty years the building was to serve as courtroom, legislative hall, church, meeting hall, concert hall, and ballroom.

The royal family lived in a spacious bungalow on King Street, built of coral blocks and surrounded by a broad, cool veranda. Nearby were the royal tombs.

Homes were scattered around the city and up the lovely Nuuanu Valley where the great King's warriors had fought many years before. Many residences still had thatched roofs, but some were built of stone and lumber brought from the Pacific Coast. The most imposing home downtown was called Washington Place. It had been named by an American when it served as the United States legation. It was later to be the home of the last Queen of Hawaii, and under the American flag it was the traditional residence of the governor.

Pictures of the city drawn at this period show not only homes but also schools, churches, hospitals, and several hotels. A department store founded by a German merchant offered for sale such luxuries as parasols, bird cages, and iron bedsteads. Business houses included those of importers, medical men and dentists, jewelers, carpenters, bakers, tailors, and barbers. There were also livery stables, drugstores, coffee shops, billiard parlors, and bowling alleys. Many kinds of goods could be bought, which had been unloaded from ships coming from all parts of the civilized world.

The streets were muddy or dusty in the daytime and dark at night. The danger of fire was great. The city was proud of the volunteer fire department and its shiny engine, with its name "Honolulu" painted on the side. It carried a long hose that could shoot a stream of water sixty feet into the heart of a blazing building. But every householder had to keep two buckets handy in case of fire. On one day, for instance, eleven downtown homes went up in smoke.

Good roads outside the towns were still few and far between. Most land travel was done on foot, although people who could afford a horse loved to dash about in the saddle and run dusty races on Saturday afternoons. A horse trail led through taro patches to the seaside of Waikiki, but not a single hotel was available there for vacationers.

A road for riders of horses and mules had been carved out across the Nuuanu pass and down the steep cliffs on the way to the north side of Oahu, but for many years it was impossible for a carriage to make this trip safely. Travelers around the island would not find a single inn on the way. But owners of country homes or native shacks offered their hospitality so generously that travelers often felt they were conferring a favor by lodging in a wayside house. The roads were slow but safe. "The stranger may travel from one end of the group to the other," wrote the chief justice, "over mountains and through woods, sleeping in grass huts, unarmed, alone, and unprotected, with any amount of treasure on his person."

People still preferred to travel by sea if they could, in canoes or on trading vessels. But journeys by sea were often long, rough, and crowded. Passengers jammed in smelly, narrow cabins of interisland schooners were often forced to seek air on the narrow decks, where they lurched about among steerage passengers and piled cargo. On one trip a little schooner brought back from the Big Island 190 passengers, 20 turkeys, 30 pigs, 75 chickens, 30 dogs, a pair of oxen, a mule, 14 cords of wood, and 11 canoes!

Small ships carried sugar, molasses, wheat, and firewood among the islands. But several fine American-built vessels were soon proudly cruising Hawaiian waters. In 1853 a company put into operation a small side-wheel steamer named *Akamai*, a name meaning "skillful" or "clever."

Honolulu was linked with the rest of the world by famous clipper ships, which often sailed regularly to the United States and British ports. And in 1854 a trial voyage was made by a pioneering steamship line.

Mail service between Hawaii and the rest of the world was still tiresomely slow. Letters might take a year or two to arrive from New York. They would be carried around Cape Horn on sailing ships and forwarded from Chile, Tahiti, or Australia. The latest European news might even arrive by way of China! Until 1846, the Hawaiian government did not offer any mail service whatever. Merchant ships carried the mails free. When a ship came into Honolulu, bags of letters and newspapers would be dumped on the floor of a shipping agent's office, and everybody who expected letters would gather round and sort out his own.

But around the middle of the century, improvement in shipping between Hawaii and California brought the mails quicker than the old-timers would have thought possible. A speed record was set in 1855 between New York and Honolulu— thirty-five days. Nowadays, jet planes can carry a letter over the same distance in less than half a day.

A central post office was set up in Honolulu in 1850. A year later the cost of a letter was reduced from ten cents to five, and the postmaster issued stamps with values of two, five, and thirteen cents. These "Missionary" issues are rare and are prized today by stamp collectors. For ten years, letters sent inside the kingdom were delivered free, to encourage the Hawaiians to write to each other often.

When Kamehameha III died in 1854, after almost thirty years on the throne, his kingdom had become a thriving Pacific crossroads. Childless, he willed his kingship to his nephew, Prince Alexander Liholiho, who took the title of Kamehameha IV.

The new King was almost twenty-one when he came to the throne in 1855. He was tall, slim, and handsome. He had visited Europe and America along with his elder brother and Dr. Judd, and spoke English as well as Hawaiian. Kamehameha IV was well educated in other ways, and had served for three years as a member of the Privy Council, so that he was trained to take over his new duties. He was hard-working and intelligent, but he was bothered by attacks of asthma. He once took some lessons from an American boxer in the hope that they would improve his health.

Young Kamehameha IV was more friendly toward English ideas than American ones. He had been brought up at a school for chiefs which was taught by Yankee missionaries, and was bored with prayer meetings. On his tour of the United States with Dr. Judd, he had once been insulted by a railway conductor, who mistook the dark-skinned Hawaiian lad for a Negro and ordered him out of the car. His anger at racial prejudice of this sort was reinforced by his fear that the United States might someday annex the Hawaiian Islands. Therefore, although some of his best friends were Americans, he slowly swung away from their advice, and at the end of his reign not one of them was in his cabinet. On the other hand, he admired the English, and his nine-year reign was marked by a revival of British influence in the kingdom.

This influence was deepened when Kamehameha IV was married at a big ceremony at Kawaiahao Church in 1856. His bride was Emma, a Hawaiian girl of high birth who was also granddaughter of old John Young, British adviser to Kamehameha the Great. She had been adopted as a child by an English doctor, had enjoyed a careful upbringing, and had gone to the same chiefs' children's school as her future husband. The wedding service was in the style of the Church of England.

The marriage was clearly a love match. The young couple fondly called each other "Aleck" and "Emma." Their little court was a dignified and gracious center of the life of Hawaii. An American physician remarked: "The King has excellent judgment, good taste, kindness of manner, and affability in social life; and on occasions of state a calm, thoughtful, self-possessed, gentlemanly, and impressive deportment, commanding respect and admiration."

The happiest event of their lives was the birth in 1858 of a little son. The child was called Albert Edward Kauikeaouli and was proclaimed heir to the throne under the title of "His Royal Highness the Prince of Hawaii." The little prince was bright and charming, but his body was frail.

The King and Queen were strongly aware that their people were dwindling under poor health conditions in the kingdom. They decided to try to set up better medical services for poor Hawaiians. Thousands had died in epidemics, and others were ill and unattended by doctors. In 1859 the King got the legislature to pass a law setting up a hospital on each of the four main islands. He himself went about Honolulu with hand outstretched, asking for contributions of money to build a hospital in Oahu. Businessmen, whaling captains, and ladies at tea parties subscribed enough to begin the erection of the Queen's Hospital, which still preserves in Honolulu the name of the tenderhearted Queen Emma.

The King and Queen also became strongly interested in religion. The result was the beginning of the Episcopal Church in Hawaii.

Both the American and English branches of the Church were invited to take part in the effort, but the Bishop of California could not spare any workers. Through the interest of

Queen Victoria, the Church of England sent out a bishop to set up a diocese in Hawaii.

The arrival of Bishop T. N. Staley was eagerly awaited in Honolulu by the King and Queen. They intended that the first ceremony would be the christening of the little prince, to whom Queen Victoria had sent a magnificent silver cup. But before the Bishop could arrive, the lovable four-year-old prince was dead of brain fever, and all Hawaii mourned.

Broken by his loss, Kamehameha IV continued to foster the "English Church." He even translated into Hawaiian the Episcopal Book of Common Prayer. But he did not live to see the laying of the cornerstone of the cathedral in 1866. Weakened by asthma and grief, his health failed, and this most brilliant of Hawaiian kings died in 1863 at the age of twenty-nine.

His elder brother, Prince Lot, was promptly proclaimed Kamehameha V. He had gained plenty of experience in practical government work. He was solemn and heavy-set, and enjoyed a quiet party at the ranch of a friend rather than the glitter of a court. He often rode horseback around the streets of Honolulu, plainly dressed and unattended. He kept a memo book of all expenses for the royal household, and each day he personally handed his servants the money needed to pay the bills due. The merchants of Honolulu had never seen a king before who was so prompt in settling his accounts.

Kamehameha V believed that the King of Hawaii should be a strong but kindly chief who would lead his people in the path he thought best for them. When a law prohibiting the Hawaiians from getting liquor was about to be repealed, he fought to keep it, saying, "I will never sign the death warrant of my people." He objected to having his subjects waste their time traveling for miles idly to watch a hula show when there was honest work to be done.

This king came to the throne in the middle of the American

Civil War. His brother had wisely proclaimed a policy of neutrality between the claims of North and South. Some people in Washington might have worried about the possibility that the pro-British leanings of the Hawaiian kings meant a dislike of America. But both the Americans and the Hawaiians tried to maintain good relations. As a friendly act, President Abraham Lincoln in 1863 raised the status of the American representative in Honolulu to that of "minister resident."

Kamehameha V feared that events were pushing his people too fast toward broad democracy and a breakup of the kingdom he had inherited from his royal forebears. He felt that he should rule as his grandfather, Kamehameha the Great, had done. His efforts to restore the personal power of the throne often aroused strong opposition, but he sincerely felt that what he did was for the highest good of his people.

He refused from the first to take the usual oath to support the Constitution of 1852, feeling that it limited his authority too greatly. He thought that nobody should vote who was uneducated or who had no land, for such people would be at the mercy of vote-chasing demagogues anxious to change the good old Hawaiian ways. When, after five weeks of debate, a constitutional convention that he had called was unable to agree, Kamehameha V personally proclaimed a new Constitution of 1864.

His opponents pointed out that if the King could give the people a constitution he could take it away again at any time. But surprisingly, the Constitution of 1864 worked fairly well, and lasted longer than any other in Hawaiian history.

The fifth Kamehameha, like his brother, reigned nine years. He was known as "the Bachelor King," for he never married. An hour before his death in 1872, he called to his bedside a sweetheart of his youth, Bernice Pauahi, who like himself was a descendant of Kamehameha the Great. She had chosen to marry Charles Reed Bishop, an enterprising young man from New York State, who had come to Honolulu to begin an outstanding career in business and banking. On his deathbed Kamehameha V asked Mrs. Bishop to serve as his successor, but she modestly declined the honor.

Mrs. Bishop had supplied from her funds the money to build the Royal Mausoleum in Nuuanu Valley, where all the kings and queens after Kamehameha I were entombed. And there was carried, to rest beside that of his brother, the coffin of Lot Kamehameha, "the last great chief of the olden type." The line of Kamehameha the Great would never again hold the throne of the Hawaiian kingdom.

The Changing Life of the Land

MANY CHANGES CAME TO HAWAII IN THE REIGNS OF THE LAST
Kamehamehas.

The school pattern changed. The missionaries had brought
reading and writing to the Island people to help them learn to
be better Christians. The mission schools by 1832 had taught
half the population to read. But by then the novelty had worn
off, and it was clear that education, especially that of children,
would have to be taken over by the government.

A law was passed in 1840 setting up common schools in
every community. A few years later a Department of Public
Instruction was formed, headed by a cabinet member. The
first one chosen was the chiefs' friend William Richards. That
was the beginning of the widespread Hawaiian school system
of later years.

By the middle of the century, most Hawaiians could read and write in their own language. Many of them wished to have their children taught English, which long before then had become the main language of business and government. The missionary view, though, was that in order to preserve the Hawaiian nation, its speech must also be preserved. All instruction in the common schools had been carried on in Hawaiian, and even in the missionary high school at Lahainaluna, Maui, no English was taught before 1846.

The Hawaiian legislature in 1853 decided that certain schools should start the study of English. Some years later, the Hawaiian language was abandoned as the medium of instruction. For at least a century, English has been the main language in Hawaii inside and outside the schools. Thus it was not too difficult to Americanize the Islands when the time came.

During the middle years there was progress in general in public education toward a modern system in keeping with American ideals of democracy, for many teachers were Americans. The system worked. In 1873 a visiting English lady noted: "I suppose there is not a better educated country in the world."

Several "select" schools had started, which were taken over by the government. One of these was the missionary boarding school for young chiefs, started in 1839. No fewer than five of the pupils afterwards sat on the throne of Hawaii. In 1846 it became the select "Royal School." Other boarding schools included one for boys at Hilo and one for girls at Wailuku, Maui.

A school for the education of missionary children was opened in 1841 in Honolulu. It grew steadily and in 1853 expanded under the name of Punahou School and Oahu College. During the gold-rush days in California, parents there sent their children over the Pacific to go to school at Punahou. After more than a century, Punahou proudly calls itself the "oldest high school west of the Rocky Mountains."

The high school at Lahainaluna had been founded by the missionaries primarily to train native teachers and pastors. During the reign of Kamehameha III, it was the leading school in the kingdom, but it cost much money and in 1849 was also transferred to the government. Lahainaluna, like the Honolulu mission, operated a busy printing press. By 1842, these two printing houses had turned out about a hundred million pages printed in Hawaiian.

Christianity was now the main religion of the Islanders. The chief types were Protestant, including both the New England Congregational and the English Episcopal varieties, and Catholic. The Catholics also operated schools, and they set up a seminary in 1846 on the windward side of Oahu to train teachers.

Another American sect began missionary work during these years. They were the Latter-day Saints, or Mormons. The first Mormon missionaries arrived in the Islands at the end of 1850. They were ten young men from the California gold camps. They soon decided that they should learn Hawaiian and work closely with the native people. Almost from the beginning they appointed Hawaiians to various offices in the Mormon Church. By 1854 they had printed a translation of the Book of Mormon and had made converts in all parts of the kingdom.

After a period of troubles within the church, the Mormons gathered at Laie on the north shore of Oahu. There the members settled and cultivated gardens, caught fish, raised cattle, and started growing broad fields of sugar cane. After a few years they began to thrive, and the money they made helped to support Mormon mission work on other islands and in several other parts of the Pacific. The Mormon Temple at Laie, dedicated in 1919, is a show place and a center of church life for a wide area.

The social life of Hawaii was lively, not only at the royal court but also in the city of Honolulu. People enjoyed dining and dancing, visiting aboard ships in the harbor, Sunday-school strawberry festivals, moonlight rides on horseback, sewing bees, agricultural fairs, cards, and charades. Nearly every foreign household had a piano and a sewing machine. It was fashionable to go to the new photographic studio and have one's picture taken, to be put in a gold locket, hung on a chain, and presented to a friend.

A number of clubs and friendly societies had been started, like those in any American city. The residents were able from time to time to see a visiting circus or minstrel show or fire-works display, or to attend a lecture, concert, debate, or ama-teur play. A special treat was a Hawaiian feast, or *luau*.

The first public theater opened in 1847 in a small adobe building. The interest was so great that money was raised to erect a special edifice, which was called the Royal Hawaiian Theater. It opened in 1848, and its first season was cut short because many actors and audience members departed to hunt gold in California. Thereafter it had a long history of staging plays. Acting companies passing through Honolulu by ship on their way to other cities of the world would often put on a play there. Other theaters opened, including one where shows were given by Chinese troupes for the growing Oriental com-munity.

Later in the century a fancy Music Hall was erected at which melodramas like *East Lynne* were played, along with such shows as *Little Lord Fauntleroy* and, of course, *Uncle Tom's Cabin*. Even grand operas were staged.

The orchestra was led by Henri Berger, brought from Germany in 1872 to head the Royal Hawaiian Band. Captain Berger served as conductor of this band for forty-three years, during which time he composed the music for seventy-five Hawaiian songs, including the national anthem, "Hawaii Ponoi" ("Our Hawaii"). He is said to have popularized European music to a point where happy Hawaiians whistled grand-opera airs as they pounded their daily poi.

More and more visitors were coming to see what they could see in the island kingdom, now to be reached by steamship. One of the most amusing visitors was a lanky, talkative fellow named Sam Clemens, who arrived in 1866 to write a series of sketches for a California newspaper. Better known by his pen name Mark Twain, he was an untiring sight-seer. He rode around on a swayback old horse, chatting with everybody he met. During his stay of four months he visited most of the landmarks in the Islands. His Hawaiian experience not only provided material for twenty-five letters to his paper, but gave Mark Twain a new profession. His famous speech on the Hawaiian Islands was his mainstay when he embarked on the career of platform lecturer, and was his favorite for more than seven years. Mark Twain's tribute to Hawaii is often quoted —"the loveliest fleet of islands that lies anchored in any ocean."

A number of other notable visitors came in the latter half of the century, and more than a hundred of them wrote books which portrayed Hawaiian scenes and scenery. Many gave good descriptions of native customs and sports, such as riding the waves on surfboards.

The beginnings of the modern tourist industry date from the time of Kamehameha V, when curious travelers, vacationists, and seekers after health and sunshine began arriving on every steamship.

The high point of every tour was a visit to the volcano region. There the traveler could easily believe that every one of the Hawaiian Islands was the top of a giant volcano, rising from the ocean's bed. The Big Island is actually formed of five volcanoes. Tallest is Mauna Kea, "White Mountain," rising six miles above the ocean floor, looming behind the town of Hilo, its top frosted with snow during part of each year. Almost as tall and much broader is Mauna Loa, "Long Mountain," whose titanic dome is topped by dozens of cones that can still spout fire fountains every few years.

The first foreigner to climb to the top of Mauna Loa was a missionary, in 1824. A year later a visiting scientist measured its height as almost fourteen thousand feet. Since that time, Mauna Loa has erupted, on an average, once every three and a half years. In that time it has added to the bulk of the Big Island about four billion cubic yards of lava.

Even more popular as a sight-seer's goal was the volcano of Kilauea, to the east of Mauna Loa, at an elevation of four thousand feet. Kilauea and its fire pit, Halemaumau, sacred to the Hawaiian goddess Pele, had long been visited, with awe and trembling, by generations of natives. The region had first been studied by scientists with Lord Byron, the British sea captain who had brought back the bodies of Kamehameha II and his Queen. Many trips to Kilauea were made by missionaries, such as the Reverend Titus Coan.

The first foreign ladies to visit Kilauea were two missionary wives in 1828, and thereafter many tourists came to see the crater and its molten beds of lava. In 1861 a noted British traveler, Lady Jane Franklin, ascended from Hilo with her niece. The two ladies rode in style in litters slung on poles between two Hawaiian bearers. They spent two nights sleeping in a grass hut on the lip of the crater. One day, wearing bloomers, they climbed down and peered over the edge of the fiery cauldron, where a priest of Pele reeled off a prayer to the goddess as the fountains flamed in the air.

An inn was built on the rim of Kilauea in 1865. Since that time there has always been a comfortable hotel at this spot, now to be reached from Hilo by automobile in less than an hour.

Although both Mauna Loa and Kilauea have erupted many times since the day in 1790 when a third of Keoua's army were killed, Pele has always given enough warning so that not one human life has been lost by volcanic action in Hawaii. In fact, Hawaii is probably the only place in the world where spectators rush to the scene of a volcanic eruption instead of fleeing away from it in terror. For more than a century, travel writers have vied with each other in trying to portray the beauties and splendors of this volcanic region.

The coming of more and more tourists made pressing the need for a good hotel in Honolulu. Only the government could afford to spend the required money, and even so, there was much objection when the huge sum of $110,000 was expended to build a modern structure on Hotel Street near the palace. Later called the Royal Hawaiian Hotel, the building was advertised in glowing terms: "All the chambers are large and airy, and fitted with luxurious baths and other modern conveniences."

During these same middle years the government spent about a million dollars on other public improvements. Most important was a large office building called Aliiolani Hale. People complained when taxes were increased to cover expenditures on Iolani Barracks, a new prison, the post office, customhouses, schools, harbor improvements, a quarantine building, and an insane asylum. The city was really spreading out.

Many Hawaiians, though, still lived in grass-roofed small houses on their old allotments of land, as they had done for centuries. But the effect of the newcomers' ways were sometimes marked, particularly in dress. Hawaiian ladies had a hard time squeezing into corsets and tight, flowing dresses of European mode.

One missionary noted that "at Honolulu, before pants came into general use among the natives, those who took in clothes of foreigners to wash made quite an income by hiring them out to unpantalooned and unclothed natives to be married in, the owners of the clothes being ignorant of the whole matter." One happy bridegroom was married in a rig consisting of a green overcoat, a starched dickey, and a pair of huge rubber boots.

The Hawaiians seldom wore shoes while on the road, but carried them in their hands until they arrived at a house. When they did wear shoes, they wore only the best—which meant the ones with the loudest squeak. The Hawaiians got the idea that a loud creaking noise was the main purpose for wearing shoes. One native agreed to pay the shoemaker as much as a dollar extra if a really tremendous squeak could be built in.

The life of the average Hawaiian at home in 1872 was not too unhappy. He still practiced his ancient arts of fishing, planting taro and making poi, and weaving mats. A man could support himself and his family by working two days a week. He could easily earn the five or ten dollars a year needed to pay taxes. The Hawaiian still enjoyed resting in the shade, chatting with friends, playing cards, reading the newspaper, and, for excitement, attending a *luau*, or feast, or taking part in an election campaign. The life of such a Hawaiian was not the same as that of a New England farmer, but it compared very favorably with the lot of many a common man in Europe at that time.

Foreign germs still continued to cut down the Hawaiian population. The worst of these germs came from China and caused leprosy, which spread to all parts of the Islands. It was believed that the only way to check the disease was to isolate all the sufferers. A law was passed to set up a receiving station in Honolulu, and those who were judged to be incurable were sent to a village on a jutting peninsula of the island of Molokai.

By 1873 about eight hundred patients, most of them Hawaiians, were settled there. These people, who sometimes included healthy folk who refused to be separated from a suffering husband or wife, were tended by workers under the Board of Health. Spiritual comfort was given by volunteer Catholic priests who kept a little chapel in the settlement. Most celebrated of these devoted men was Father Joseph Damien de Veuster of Belgium. Father Damien himself finally caught the lingering disease, of which he died a martyr's death in 1889. Today, fortunately, modern methods of treatment have nearly wiped out the dread disease, and only a few people still dwell in the village on the barren north shore of Molokai.

Cowboys and Cane Raisers

YOU MIGHT NOT THINK OF A PACIFIC ISLAND AS A SPOT WHERE
a cattle ranch can be found. But Hawaiian cowboys were las-
soing wild bulls and branding mavericks many years before the
cattle business was an important part of the American West.

The longhorn cattle brought from California in 1793 by
Captain Vancouver were protected by a *kapu* laid on them
by King Kamehameha I. Since none were killed, they multi-
plied and ran wild. In some places they ate up the forest cover
and trampled the taro patches of the Hawaiians. An American
named John Palmer Parker, as has been told, in 1815 was
given by the King the job of shooting the extra cattle, preparing their hides for shipment, and salting the beef for sale to
visiting ships. Through many years, Mr. Parker built up a
ranch which today is still running, and which is one of the
largest under the American flag.

A Hawaiian chief visited California in the early years and persuaded some Spanish cowboys to go to the Big Island and teach the people how to ride and rope. They took with them their high-horned saddles and long spurs and braided lassos. The Hawaiian lads found it was fun to learn the ranch hand's trade, and soon were galloping about the Hawaiian range like real buckaroos. The Hawaiian word for cowboy is still *paniolo*, taken from *español*, or Spaniard, the first kind of cowboy in the Islands.

The King let out on contract the right to kill the wild herds. "Bullock hunters" roamed the Waimea hills in the 1840's. Some were Californians, who wore ponchos and used Spanish saddles and spurs in their roping work. Wild bulls were trapped in pits dug along the trails. Sometimes an unlucky man might fall into a pit and be gored to death by a trapped animal.

Gradually the wild beasts were thinned out, and improved breeds of stock were settled on ranches. About two thousand hides were exported every year, and the carcasses were boiled down for tallow. As late as 1875, hides and tallow were of greater value than the meat, but today all the cattle in Hawaii do not begin to supply the local demand for meat. About a fourth of the entire land area in the Islands is used for pasture, mostly for cattle.

The Hawaiian cowboy's working outfit was fully as colorful as that of the American cowboy. The *paniolo* wore a huge sombrero of woven pandanus, decked with a *lei* of fresh flowers. He wore a red kerchief at his neck and a red sash around his waist. His shirt was a blue cotton plaid, especially made for the Island trade. His high leather leggings not only protected him from thorny brush but also served as a sheath for his long knife. On one side of this fine steel knife were sharp saw teeth. When an animal was first lassoed and while the clever pony held the rope taut, the cowboy leaped down and quickly sawed off the pointed horns so that no one would be injured when the wild beast was driven to a fenced pasture.

Special spurs that made a pretty jingling sound were worn by the *paniolo*. His best trousers were of white cloth, and at the roundup—a social event witnessed by high chiefs and even the royal family—the proud cowboy rode and roped all day in white trousers. If at the end of the rodeo he had not been thrown and his pants showed only rope marks, the cowpuncher was rewarded by a *lei* from the queen of the ceremony.

Many mainland rodeo events have been won by *paniolos* from Hawaii. One of them twice beat the world champion roper by tying up an animal in one minute flat. Another cowboy, grandson of the founder of the Parker Ranch, was unlucky enough to lose a hand in a roping accident, but he won fame as the one-armed champion roper of the world.

The cowboys of Hawaii had to know how to ride the waves as well as ride the hills. For many years, the cattle raised on the island of Maui, in the lee of the gigantic crater called the "House of the Sun," were shipped to market on a steamer that anchored in a shallow bay. The mounted cowboy would rope a bellowing steer by the horns and ride into the surf. Then, dodging sharks, he would pass the rope to a sailor in a whaleboat. When eight animals were thus held, the boat would be hauled out to the ship, with cattle swimming on each side. They would then be slung aboard and sent off to market on the deck of the puffing steamer.

During the reigns of the last Kamehamehas, the whaling trade, which had been the mainstay of commerce before that time, was dying out. In the best year, 1852, the whaleships brought almost 375,000 barrels of oil into Hawaiian ports. Twenty years later the catch had dropped to 20,000.

A number of the whalers were owned by Hawaiian subjects. The first that flew the flag of the kingdom was the *Denmark Hill*, fitted out in 1832. But the heyday of the Hawaiian whalers came in the 1850's and 1860's. In 1862 and 1863 the brig *Kohala* hunted far to the north. She wintered in the Arctic seas and brought back a good catch, although her captain was killed by a treacherous Eskimo.

It was not always necessary to go to the icy waters of the north to kill whales. Several businessmen set up whaling stations on the south shore of the island of Maui. This custom of "bay whaling," as it was called, was quite profitable. In 1870 a whale ship shot two hundred of the sea beasts with a newly invented whale gun. But soon after that, the whales decided to stay away from the bays of Maui, and shore-based hunting died out.

Around the world the whaling industry, which had been of great value to Americans as well as Hawaiians, was petering out, for several reasons. One was that so many whales had been killed. In less than forty years, almost three hundred thousand whales were slaughtered around the globe. The business of hunting them from cruising sailing ships was wasteful. Often, for every three whales killed, two would be lost before they could be brought to the ship's side. Other causes were the need for longer and longer voyages, and thus heavier expenses for refitting far from home; the rising cost of ships; and the lack of skilled seamen to seek out the whales and hurl the harpoon. The life of a whaler was so harsh that, particularly in the Pacific, many sailors deserted. Toward the end of the whaling era, desertions in Hawaii were so frequent that the captains would pay rewards to people who would catch escaping sailors and bring them back to their ships.

Another reason why people would not pay high prices for whale oil for their lamps was the discovery of petroleum in

Pennsylvania in 1859. Kerosene and illuminating gas were thereafter preferred for lighting purposes.

The Civil War was hard on whaleships. Forty of them were sunk to make one barricade off South Carolina. Confederate privateers sank fifty more. One of these, the *Shenandoah*, preyed on whalers in the Pacific even after the war was officially over. On one day this privateer captured eleven ships. Most of them were burned, while their helpless crews watched with rage as their hard-earned treasure went up in oily flames. The *Shenandoah* destroyed twenty-five ships of the Arctic fleet, at least three of them Hawaii-owned vessels.

After the war, the main hunting ground was the cold and foggy region north of Bering Strait. Several times the ships stayed late in the fall, running the risk of being frozen into the ice. In the terrible year 1871, more than thirty whale ships, seven of them Hawaiian, were caught in the ice and either crushed or else held so fast that they had to be abandoned. The crews, including some women and children, walked southward down the coast and made their way in open whaleboats through choppy seas to board a few ships that had not been trapped in the ice pack.

Amazingly, not one life was lost, but the whaling fleet never recovered from the blow. Seven years later a similar disaster, in which thirteen ships were lost and fifty people were killed, put a finish to the importance of whaling for the businessmen of Hawaii.

The decline of the whaling trade was slow. Fortunately, there was time to make up for the loss by the growth of new sources of income. Chief among these was agriculture.

The rise of a plantation economy in Hawaii was not rapid. Various crops were tried out.

Coffee trees were grown in Manoa Valley near Honolulu as early as 1825. Missionaries began growing coffee a few years later on Kauai and in the Kona region of the Big Island. They were plagued by labor troubles, drought, flood, and an insect blight; but finally the growers around Kona were successful. The industry has continued there until today, and the strong, high-quality Kona coffee is Hawaii's third most valuable crop. Harvesting is so important that the school children of Kona are let out in the fall to help pick the coffee crop. They make up for lost time by going to school until August the following year.

Wheat, potatoes, rice, tobacco, indigo, peanuts, oranges, and cotton were at various times tried as staple crops. Silk production was another experiment. On the island of Kauai, mulberry trees were planted for feed, silkworm eggs were brought in from China and America, and Hawaiians were taught to tend the cocoonery. But again, labor troubles, drought, high winds, and insect pests caused heavy losses, and the idea was given up.

A strange export during the middle years was pulu, a fuzzy fiber stripped from the base of tree-fern fronds. It was found to be excellent stuffing for pillows and mattresses. The gathering of this pulu in the damp forests of the Big Island was hard work for the poor laborers, who could earn only about four dollars for a hundredweight of the stuff.

Small quantities of fruits, vegetables, and spices were shipped abroad or sold to visiting ships. A few pineapples were also exported, but the fruit was not of the best quality. The prime product of Hawaiian planters, as it turned out, was sugar cane, which is still the biggest money crop in the Fiftieth State.

The sweet story of sugar in Hawaii starts with Captain Cook, who saw cane fields which had been planted by natives, on which they fattened their hogs. A number of early writers predicted that the refining of sugar and distilling of rum from molasses would bring fortune to the Islanders. But the way to wealth was long and hard, and rum was never made commercially.

A Chinese named Wong Tze Chun on the island of Lanai, it is said, produced a little sugar as early as 1802, on a crude stone mill brought from his homeland. Marín the Spaniard manufactured some in 1819. Early methods were very primitive. The natives would crush the cane stalks by beating them on poi boards, and then slowly boil the juice in a copper kettle.

The first serious effort to start a plantation was made about 1835 on the island of Kauai, where an American firm named Ladd & Company leased a tract at Koloa. After heartbreaking labors in getting started, they produced about two tons of sugar and twenty-seven hundred gallons of molasses. The sugar was not of good quality. The first mill was a crude press whose wooden rollers wore out very soon. Iron rollers worked better, and within a few years an improved mill, run by water power, came into operation. The plantation struggled on for years until in 1848 the energetic Dr. R. W. Wood took it over and gave it a strong management. Koloa Plantation is still producing sugar today.

Mills were set up after 1838 in various parts of the kingdom, by missionaries and others, to grind cane on shares for native growers. In 1836 only four tons of sugar were exported. But at the end of the reign of Kamehameha V the output averaged almost a thousand tons a year. This figure is trifling in comparison with the production of later years, but it brought a new economic life to the land of the Kamehamehas.

There were many ups and downs. Growers tried to expand too rapidly, and their firms failed. There were business depressions in some years. The lack of a steady supply of low-priced labor grew serious. But in spite of such troubles, the sugar industry went ahead and brought a golden prosperity to the Islands.

Part of the success of the sugar growers was due to improvements in growing and milling. A deep plow was devised by one of the men at Koloa to improve planting methods. A centrifugal machine for separating sugar from molasses was worked out by David M. Weston in 1851. This "whirl-dry" method did well in a few minutes what had formerly taken weeks to do poorly. The vacuum pan, which enabled the mill to boil sugar at a lower temperature and without scorching, was introduced early in the 1860's. Steam power was applied to mills, using as fuel the pressed, dried cane stalks. Thus the cane plant provided not only the sugar syrup but the fuel to refine that syrup. Hawaiian sugar came to be of such a high grade that it could be sold to groceries for table use without being further treated. It was not only shipped to other countries but sold to local dealers and visiting ships.

The ancient Hawaiian custom of irrigating the fields was revived by the sugar planters. Few plantations could operate without irrigation, since no less than four thousand tons of water are needed to grow enough cane to make one ton of sugar!

A ten-mile ditch was dug in 1856 to supply the Lihue Plantation on Kauai. The biggest early irrigation project was the Hamakua Ditch on the island of Maui, designed to bring water from the wet northern slopes of Mount Haleakala around its flanks to the sunbaked central plain. Two partners, S. T. Alexander and H. P. Baldwin, both sons of missionaries, borrowed money and began work in 1876.

To get the water across the ravines on the slopes, large and heavy pipes had to be laid down each side and across each deep gash in the earth, to make an upside-down siphon. The final canyon, the Maliko Gorge, was so dismaying that it seemed the effort must fail. The workers needed to lower themselves on ropes down a steep cliff. They refused to do this. The work stopped.

Then Manager Baldwin decided to show them the way. He had lost one of his arms in a mill accident, but this did not stop him. He used his legs to slide down the rope and then, with his one arm, he alternately gripped and released the rope and grabbed a new hold lower down. Shamed by this show of courage by a one-armed man, the workers followed Baldwin. To keep them heartened and to inspect the work, Baldwin went through his daring trick day after day until the gorge was bridged.

The Hamakua Ditch, when finished in 1878, ran for seventeen miles and delivered forty million gallons of water a day. But even bigger ditches were soon built in the same region, until the desert plain was covered with acres of waving green cane. Great as they seemed at the time, the earlier irrigation projects were surpassed. One modern ditch carries sixty million gallons daily through ten miles of tunnel. The building of great reservoirs to hold water until needed has created man-made lakes on several of the Islands.

Underground supplies of water were tapped by artesian wells as early as 1879. Ewa Plantation on the island of Oahu now has sixty such wells, which daily pump forth for irrigating use almost enough water to supply the needs of a modern city the size of San Francisco.

Kings Elected by the People

KING KAMEHAMEHA V DIED UNEXPECTEDLY IN 1872, AT THE very time when the nation was celebrating his forty-third birthday. He had never formally named a successor. The people decided that, since they had not inherited a king, they would elect one by vote.

Never before had the subjects of the kingdom had a chance to decide who should be their ruler. The two most likely candidates were William Charles Lunalilo and David Kalakaua. Their champions started a busy campaign.

Prince William, as he was called, was very popular because of his personality, his liberal ideas, and his high birth. He was a descendant of a half brother of Kamehameha I. There is a story that at his christening his mother told the Reverend

Hiram Bingham that the baby should be called Lunalilo, meaning "Most High in Rank."

David Kalakaua was not a member of the Kamehameha line, but of a family who had been leaders on the Big Island for generations. It was said that they were descended from a chief brought from Tahiti in the South Seas to rule Hawaii in ancient times. David in 1863 had married the lovely Kapiolani. She was the granddaughter of King Kaumualii, rival of Kamehameha I. Through his wife, Kalakaua was thus linked to the royal family of the island of Kauai.

The campaign was hot on both sides. Prince Lunalilo issued a message to the people, promising to restore the Constitution of 1852 and to rule as a liberal monarch under it. The Kalakaua side circulated a paper which tried to show that Lunalilo did not really belong to the Kamehameha line. Kalakaua charged that Lunalilo had been misled by foreigners, and promised that if he, Kalakaua, were elected, he would repeal all personal taxes and put native Hawaiians into government jobs.

The attack on Lunalilo's birth was so much resented that the people at a mass meeting instructed their representatives to vote for Lunalilo and nobody else. Thus the final votes on January 8, 1873, were all for William C. Lunalilo, and next day at Kawaiahao Church he was proclaimed the new King.

Lunalilo, the people's choice, had been brought up as a darling of the nobility. He was a fine-looking man of thirty-eight when he came to the throne, tall, broad-chested, and aristocratic. He could feel at home not only with Hawaiians but with foreigners of the highest class.

King Lunalilo began at once to do several things. He started to change the constitution to abolish the property qualification of voters. And, like his two predecessors, he tried to obtain a treaty with the United States that would be more favorable to the sugar growers of Hawaii. The kingdom was feeling a depression, and more income was badly needed. As an inducement to the people of America to accept such a treaty favoring Hawaii, the idea arose that a lease on Pearl Harbor near Honolulu might be offered to America for a naval station. A storm of protest arose against this scheme and it was rejected. The United States was finally given these rights fifteen years later.

The King's main defect was a lack of decision, which, had he lived longer, might have brought harm to his kingdom. This weakness was revealed when a mutiny broke out among the sixty soldiers of the Household Troops, the only army the kingdom owned. One Sunday they rebelled and knocked down their drillmaster, a captain from Hungary. They then locked themselves in Iolani Barracks and refused to submit even to the strongest orders.

Finally the King sent them a message to go home, which they slowly obeyed. Then he disbanded this expensive troop, which had little to do except guard some buildings and march in parades. But the King's failure to put down mutiny at once could easily have led to a dangerous race riot, Hawaiian soldiers *vs.* foreigners. It was suspected that David Kalakaua, for his own ends, was stirring up the mutineers.

The King's health was poor and during the year became worse. It was clear that he had tuberculosis. But he felt that he was recovering and refused to name a successor, insisting that the people should name their king as they had named him.

The election of representatives to the legislative assembly was set for February 2, 1874. The vote showed the way the political wind was blowing. Nearly all the men chosen were native Hawaiians and members of the Kalakaua faction. The next evening a bugle call from the barracks sounded the sad news. Lunalilo had died, after a reign of one year and twenty-five days.

King Lunalilo was laid out in state for three weeks, wrapped in his cloak of golden feathers. He was buried, not in the Royal Mausoleum, but next to his mother in the graveyard of Kawaiahao Church. Thus passed the "Kind Chief," first of Hawaii's elected kings.

The stormy reign of the second one was ushered in by a stormy election. David Kalakaua announced his new candidacy the day after Lunalilo died. This time his opponent was Queen Dowager Emma, widow of Kamehameha IV. She had been living quietly since returning in 1866 from a trip to Europe, where she had enjoyed the friendship of Queen Victoria in England.

The contest promised to be bitter. The support of the native Hawaiians was about equally divided between Kalakaua and Emma. It was felt that she would try to restore the influence of England in Hawaiian affairs, and hence most Americans were strong for Kalakaua.

On the day of the election, the courthouse was surrounded by crowds of Hawaiians, most of them supporters of Emma. They feared that the legislators might not vote fairly. When it was announced that Kalakaua had received thirty-nine votes against only six for Emma, angry cries arose.

Three committeemen left the courthouse on their way to announce to David Kalakaua that he was King of Hawaii. As they stepped into their carriage, the crowd attacked. The plug hats of the legislators were knocked in the gutter, their tail coats were torn off, and they were glad to rush back into the building alive.

The mob armed itself with spokes snatched from the carriage wheels, and rushed up the courthouse stairs. Two Americans held off the rioters for twenty minutes. But others climbed the outside stairs, broke through a door, and proceeded to wreck the building. Books, furniture, and public documents were thrown out the windows. Members who had voted for Kalakaua were beaten as they tried to escape; one died as a result of his injuries.

To prevent further damage the authorities, led by Kalakaua, invited armed marines from two American ships and one British ship in the harbor to land and restore order. They remained ashore for a week to maintain peace. By that time King Kalakaua was firmly on the throne. He made peace with Emma and named as his heir his popular younger brother.

"The Merry Monarch," as Kalakaua was called, was a paradox, at once kingly and democratic. Ruler by vote, he tried to restore personal power by political means, and his efforts were so violent that they resulted finally in the overthrow of the monarchy. He tried to be more of a king than many a nineteenth-century ruler who had been born to a throne.

Kalakaua was burly and his side whiskers were impressive. He could speak and write well in both English and Hawaiian. He was a trained orator and had served as a newspaper editor. He was fond of literature; his name appeared as author of the first important collection in English of legends and myths about Hawaii. He enjoyed the company of celebrated authors such as Robert Louis Stevenson. Above all, he was fond of music. He himself composed the words of "Hawaii Ponoi," the national anthem, and he liked nothing better than to listen to the concerts of the Royal Hawaiian Band.

Kalakaua Rex enjoyed the society of many kinds of men, and was genial and easy to approach. His glittering court was modeled on storybook dreams. He could represent his nation in full-dress uniform, and then relax in his boathouse, playing poker with genial foreigners. He was interested in ancient Hawaiian things and in modern science, too. The first telephone line installed on Oahu was a private wire from the palace to the boathouse, where the royal yacht awaited his pleasure. Kalakaua wanted to be a king who was really a king.

His reign started out well. He made a royal progress among the Islands, greeting his subjects and promising to work for them. And before his first year was out, he himself went to the United States to help promote the signing of a long-awaited treaty that would make King Sugar the real monarch of the Hawaiian Islands.

The story of this "reciprocity" treaty goes back to the middle of the century, when it was hoped that the United States, main market for sugar and other Hawaiian products, would agree to permit these to be marketed in the United States without a high duty. American goods could likewise be sold in Hawaii without duty.

Kalakaua's three predecessors had failed to get such a treaty. When at the request of sugar growers the legislature approved another effort, the King himself decided to go to the United States to see if he could help. He had already been thinking of visiting that big country, and it turned out to be a beneficial trip.

Never before had the king of any land visited the United States, and Kalakaua's good-will tour was a great triumph. After a royal reception when his ship reached San Francisco, the King crossed the continent in a palace car built for President Ulysses S. Grant, who greeted him in Washington. There Kalakaua was presented to both Houses of Congress. Before returning to Hawaii he toured New York and various places in New England associated with Hawaiian history—such as Boston, home of the first missionaries, and New Bedford, port of many whaleships.

The negotiators sent to Washington were finally successful in getting a treaty in 1875. It was not easy, since it seemed that most of the benefits would go to the sugar growers of

Hawaii. However, Americans had almost a monopoly of trade with the Islands, and wanted to keep it. The United States Senate insisted that the Hawaiians must not sign a similar treaty with any other country.

The reciprocity treaty thus brought Hawaii firmly into the circle of American influence, and it might be expected that thereafter the two countries would grow closer and closer. That is what happened.

The immediate effect on business in Hawaii was tremendous. Everybody began making money from sugar. Fifteen years after the treaty was signed, the tonnage of sugar shipped from Hawaii had increased ten times over. Thereafter the production doubled every ten years!

Improvements in the sugar industry helped to increase the yield. The first planters had used cuttings of native plants, and boasted that they obtained as much as four tons of cane an acre. In 1854 a better variety was imported from Tahiti in the South Seas. Many years later one of its selected descendants produced up to a hundred tons an acre.

Around the end of the century, this variety became afflicted with a baffling root rot. Scientists carrying on research for the Hawaiian Sugar Planters' Association, founded in 1895, began breeding many new varieties that would resist the disease. Out of thousands of new seedlings they developed, one of them turned out to be tougher than the rest and was widely adopted. Still better modern varieties developed by science have made Hawaiian cane yield the highest sugar content per acre in the world.

The rise of large plantations led to a closer association between the growers and the businessmen of Honolulu. The boom in Hawaiian sugar that resulted when the Civil War in America cut off the supply from Louisiana made the money-men take notice. Here, they found, was a better investment than acting as agent for whaleships! Most of the leading business houses in Hawaii started in the past century as agencies, or "factors," as they were called, for groups of sugar plantations. A number of the businessmen were sons of missionaries.

A large amount of the capital needed to finance the sugar booms was lent by Americans, some of whom settled in the Islands and added energetic leadership to the American colony there.

At the beginning of Kalakaua's reign, the population of Hawaii was at its lowest ebb. Fewer people lived there than at any time before or since. Of a total of about fifty-seven thousand, all but about five thousand were Hawaiian or part-Hawaiian. The foreigners came from "nearly every nation under heaven," as one resident remarked, but were mostly Americans and British. A growing group, however, came from China. These were immigrants brought in to work on the sugar plantations.

The need for such laborers was the origin of the polyracial complexion of Hawaii in its later years. The Hawaiians themselves could see no reason why they should spend their lives hoeing cane in the hot sun. They preferred to cling to their old ways of life and let others try to get rich raising sugar for dollars.

To do the work, it was thought at first that other South Sea Islanders should be brought to Hawaii. But they did not fill the bill either, and in all, only about twenty-five hundred of them were brought. Most of them went back to their southern islands after their terms were ended.

Bringing in labor from China's teeming population had been suggested as early as 1816. The first shipload of Chinese laborers arrived in Honolulu in 1852, on five-year contracts. Fifteen years later a total of thirteen hundred had come. Some of these workers eventually went back to China, but many stayed and married Hawaiian girls, who found John Chinaman to be a model, hard-working husband.

Such families often saved money and moved to town to start small businesses. This earliest wave of immigrants earned an increasingly important place in the Islands. Today, many persons of Chinese blood are found in all walks of life, the professions as well as agriculture and business.

The income from the sugar boom enabled Kalakaua's government to obtain more funds from taxes. Money was freer, and men gathered around the King to help him and help themselves as well. Kalakaua had a chance to live as he had dreamed a real king should live.

Fall of the
Island Kingdom

A TOUR OF THE WORLD! NO KING HAD EVER BEFORE MADE SUCH a trip. Kalakaua decided he would be the first.

To rule in his absence he left his sister, Princess Liliuokalani, who had been named heiress when the King's brother died in 1877. Accompanied by his chamberlain, his attorney general, and his valet, Kalakaua set out early in 1881.

The party first went to San Francisco, and from there took a steamer to Japan. The ruling Mikado gave Kalakaua a great welcome, for he was the first king of a Christian nation to set foot on the soil of Japan. The Japanese government, which had declined a treaty with Hawaii in 1860, had signed one in 1871. After Kalakaua's visit, the ties between the two island kingdoms were to become closer. In fact, Kalakaua suggested to the Mikado a future marriage between his six-year-old niece, the lovely Princess Kaiulani, and one of the princes of Japan.

Kalakaua continued his tour through China, Siam, India, Egypt, and the great capitals of Europe. Everywhere he was royally honored and entertained. On his return to Honolulu in October he was given a grand celebration by his people.

Seeing foreign courts had given Kalakaua many new ideas about royal ceremonies. Before he left England he ordered, for himself and his Queen, two golden crowns set with precious jewels. These were to be donned at his coronation, which had been voted by the legislature in 1880, even though no previous Hawaiian ruler had ever been crowned.

The coronation was held on February 12, 1883, the ninth anniversary of Kalakaua's election. The scene was the fine new Iolani Palace, whose cornerstone had been laid in 1879. The ceremony was witnessed by representatives of all the countries with which Hawaii had official relations.

Eight thousand people gathered around the outdoor pavilion on the palace grounds. With much pomp and ceremony, Kalakaua was robed with a cloak of Kamehameha I, made of five thousand tuft feathers of the o-o bird. He stood beside a tabu stick—a seven-foot tusk of narwhal—and the kahili, the feathered pole symbolizing royal power. Then Kalakaua placed upon his own head and that of his queen, Kapiolani, the golden crowns.

The jeweled regalia were never worn again. But years later, on the night the Hawaiian monarchy was overthrown in a revolution, an officer of the Provisional Government discovered some of his soldiers throwing dice in the palace basement. The stakes were gems pried from the crown of Kalakaua Rex.

Two days after the coronation, the statue of Kamehameha the Great that still stands in front of the Aliiolani Hale office building was unveiled by Kalakaua. But the high ideals represented by this statue were not always remembered in the kingdom. Self-seeking men such as Walter Murray Gibson had won the King's confidence and proceeded to use it to gain power and money.

A large tract of plantation land was given by the legislature to a San Francisco sugar tycoon named Claus Spreckels for a low sum. The prohibition against giving liquor to Hawaiians was repealed, with sad results. Another bill gave Spreckels the right to mint silver coins bearing a bust of Kalakaua; on this deal Spreckels made a large profit. Other bills were proposed to set up a lottery, to deal in opium, and to sell exemptions to lepers, so that they would escape being isolated at the Molokai settlement.

Spurred on by Gibson, King Kalakaua got the idea that he should become the head of a great Polynesian federation, consisting of all the other Pacific islands which had not yet been taken over by the great powers of the world.

To start this grandiose scheme, Kalakaua sent an envoy to Samoa. An agreement of confederation was signed with one of the Samoan chiefs. To make a show of naval power, the Hawaiian government bought and hurriedly fitted out an old trading ship, armed it with guns, and sent it to the South Pacific to demonstrate Hawaii's military might. But the crew mutinied, and the officers brought disgrace rather than honor to their flag. And Kalakaua's dream of heading all the Pacific islanders clashed with the iron intentions of big powers such as Germany. He had to slink off the international stage, and his dream of a league of Polynesian peoples was doomed to fade away.

Moreover, scandal and corruption in his own islands threatened Kalakaua with the loss of his own powers. Early in 1887 a secret organization called the Hawaiian League had been formed to fight for a more liberal constitution than the one which permitted Kalakaua to play politics. Hundreds of Islanders joined the movement. The league members obtained guns and ammunition, and were prepared to fight if necessary to obtain their rights. If the King's powers were not limited by a new constitution, then the monarchy would have to be overthrown and a republic set up.

The immediate cause of the Revolution of 1887 was a case of bribery in which the King himself was involved. Instead of passing out rifles and marching on the palace, however, the aroused citizens held a big mass meeting. Unanimous resolutions were passed, demanding that the King dismiss his corrupt cabinet and other officials, and that he promise never again to interfere in politics.

Bloodshed was avoided by this popular show of strength. Most of Kalakaua's troops had deserted him. Hurriedly he appointed a new cabinet, which drew up a more liberal constitution, which he signed on July 6. Gibson was arrested on charges of embezzlement but allowed to leave for San Francisco. The battered warship was recalled from Samoan waters. Henceforth Kalakaua would have to play a more subdued role as King of the Hawaiian Islands.

The ousting of Gibson made possible the renewal of the reciprocity treaty, which was up for reconsideration. Negotiations had been stalled because the American Congress felt that the United States was not getting any advantages from the treaty and that Hawaiian plantations were competing with mainland sugar growers.

The Senate on January 20, 1887, inserted an amendment to read that Hawaii would give the United States the "exclusive right to enter the harbor of Pearl River, in the Island of Oahu, and to establish and maintain there a coaling and repair station for the use of vessels of the United States." The reform cabinet decided to accept, and the treaty was concluded before the end of the year. The value of Pearl Harbor to the Americans was not realized at the time, though, and not till twenty years later did the United States begin to develop the Pearl Harbor naval base.

The Constitution of 1887 made some changes in the law of the land to curb the King's power, but he still could threaten to veto acts passed by the legislature. He made use of rifts in the solidity of the Reform party. Many Hawaiians were irked that the authority of their highest chief had been cut down. They were ripe for another revolution, this time against the Reform party.

The revolt of 1889 was led by a fiery Hawaiian named Robert W. Wilcox, who had studied military science in Italy on a royal scholarship. At dawn on the morning of July 30, in his cadet uniform, Wilcox at the head of about a hundred and fifty armed followers surrounded the government buildings and set up artillery.

The King retired to his boathouse, and his royal guard refused to allow the rebels to enter the palace. The cabinet acted quickly, and summoned volunteers to defend the regime. The revolutionists, after firing a burst of shrapnel at the Opera House, were driven to take refuge in a large bungalow on the palace grounds.

Sniped at all day by a band of sharpshooters, the Wilcox forces at last flew a white tablecloth from one of the bungalow windows. They had surrendered hastily when the son of the British consul general, who acted as catcher on the local baseball team, tossed some dynamite bombs on the roof of the bungalow. Seven rebels had been killed and a dozen wounded.

Wilcox was tried for treason. But he argued that he was really trying to help the King regain his old powers. The Hawaiian jury freed him on the grounds that he was acting for the King, and "the King could do no wrong."

Kalakaua still continued to seek political strength. He was aided by a party formed among the Hawaiians, which hoped to restore the Constitution of 1864. The weakened Reform party was forced to install a compromise cabinet.

At the end of the active legislative session, King Kalakaua was a sick man. Hoping that travel would improve his health, he left for California. The ceremonies in which he took part in several cities did not help his strength. He passed away in San Francisco on January 20, 1891.

One of his last acts was to speak a message to his people in Hawaiian. His words were recorded on a crude machine recently invented, the Edison phonograph. They are still to be heard today, the first recording of the voice of any king.

The first news that his people had of Kalakaua's passing came when the ship *Charleston* rounded Diamond Head with her flag at half mast and the coffin of the King aboard. After lying in state, the body was entombed in the Royal Mausoleum, and Kalakaua's sister became Queen of Hawaii. She was to be the country's last royal ruler.

Liliuokalani, whose name means "The Salt Air of Heaven," was fifty-two years old when she ascended the throne on January 29, 1891. Her features were strong and resolute. She had large, dark eyes, and her black hair was tinged with gray. Her voice was pleasant and musical, and she spoke gracefully in English as well as in Hawaiian. Her manner was that of one accustomed to rule. Like Kalakaua, she had studied at the Royal School. Shortly after birth she had been adopted by the parents of Bernice Pauahi, whom Kamehameha V had asked to succeed him on the throne, and she had been brought up as part of the social circle around the throne.

Twice she had served as Kalakaua's regent in his absence. Her ideas were similar to his, and her will was even stronger. She had married John Dominis, a sea captain from Europe who had served as governor of Oahu; but his wise counsel was lost to her when he died only seven months after she took the throne. Her desire to regain the high authority of the olden monarchs was soon to lead her into *pilikia*—trouble.

The Queen's reign suffered from hard times, resulting from an American tariff, passed in 1890, which wiped out the benefits that Hawaiian sugar growers had enjoyed before. Kalakaua's politics had alarmed the businessmen who were now the mainstay of Island prosperity. It seemed to many that the eventual destiny of Hawaii was to be annexation by the United States, her most powerful neighbor country. Island sugar producers would probably benefit if that were to happen.

The Annexation Club, a small secret organization composed mainly of residents of foreign blood, who felt that a big change offered the only hope for stable government, was formed in Honolulu in the spring of 1892. Revolution was again in the air.

The royalists in the legislature, urged on by the Queen, fought to overthrow the Constitution of 1887. They also passed a bill setting up a lottery and another permitting the sale of opium. The Queen was determined to proclaim a new constitution under which she would be able to appoint members of the upper house of the legislature and to exclude from voting rights all foreigners not married to Hawaiian women. But after she had dismissed the legislature, her own cabinet was afraid to sign the new constitution, and advised her not to proclaim it, for fear of a revolution.

She decided to wait for a while, but that same afternoon a Committee of Safety was organized to take action. Dominated by members of the Annexation Club, this group decided that there must no longer be kings or queens in Hawaii.

The revolutionists had recruited about a hundred and fifty men. They were headed by Sanford B. Dole, son of an American missionary family. When first invited to command, he had not been eager to overthrow the monarchy, but after thinking deeply he came to the decision that Liliuokalani should give up her throne and that the United States should be asked to take Hawaii under its protection.

On the afternoon of Monday, January 16, 1893, the committee arranged with the American minister in Honolulu to have troops landed from the U.S.S. *Boston,* then in the harbor, to protect American citizens and help in keeping order. Next day the committee's plans were ready.

Three o'clock was set as zero hour for taking possession of Aliiolani Hale, the government office building. The Queen was defended by the police force and her household guards, a total number about equal to that of the revolutionaries. Her marshal, learning of the plan, sent a force to defend the Hale. About a hundred Hawaiians were gathered on the steps of the Opera House nearby, and police were waiting across the street from a business house to arrest Dole and his committee when they should come out.

At two thirty a shot was fired that sounded the knell of the Hawaiian kingdom. John Good, in charge of a wagonload of ammunition leaving a hardware store, was attacked by a force of Hawaiian policemen. He fired his revolver and winged a man who was trying to grab the reins from him. The wagon dashed off and escaped with the ammunition. The Hawaiian crowd ran from the Opera House to the scene of the commotion.

Meanwhile, unarmed, Dole and his friends walked into Aliiolani Hale and ordered a few startled clerks to surrender. Then their forces seized the treasury and the archives. From the steps the committee read a proclamation ending the monarchy and setting up a Provisional Government until annexation could be arranged.

They demanded that Liliuokalani surrender her powers at once. She did so under protest, stating that since American

troops were in her capital, she was forced to "yield to the
superior force of the United States." The men from the
Boston remained ashore, and on February 1 the Stars and
Stripes were raised over Hawaii to show that it was now under
the protection of the United States of America.

Problems for President Dole

SANFORD B. DOLE, HEAD OF THE PROVISIONAL GOVERNMENT that had taken over the Islands from the Queen, was faced with many pressing problems.

The first of these was to gain recognition of his regime. Every day he wondered if the royalists would launch a battle to win back the country. A Japanese warship was in Honolulu Harbor, ready to land troops if necessary, and a British gunboat was on the way. Things were tense.

Mr. Dole at once sent five commissioners to Washington to ask that the United States annex the Islands. Their arguments won out over those of the champions of Queen Liliuokalani. A treaty of annexation was written which was signed by President Benjamin Harrison and immediately sent to the Senate.

About two weeks later, though, the United States got a new President of a different party. And Grover Cleveland, Democrat, had his doubts about taking Hawaii under the American flag. He withdrew the treaty and sent a special commissioner, James H. Blount, to Honolulu with full powers to investigate the revolution.

Three days after he arrived in Honolulu, which by now was almost an armed camp, Blount, formerly a Confederate colonel in the Civil War, ordered that the American flag be hauled down and that the troops march back on board their ships. Blount then spent several months getting information for a report to President Cleveland on the revolution that had deposed Liliuokalani.

When a copy of this report finally got back to Dole and his men of the Provisional Government, they felt that it was unjust. Blount seemed to be attacking everyone who had petitioned for annexation by the United States. The report was followed by the arrival of a new American representative in Honolulu. He carried orders to put Queen Liliuokalani back on the throne.

The officers of the Provisional Government refused to budge. They said that President Cleveland had no right to meddle in the affairs of the existing Hawaiian government. They felt that it was no longer possible to give up the progress already gained in the march toward more democratic rule in the Islands. They knew that American warships would never fire on a government that was seeking annexation by America. They were right. Congress decided that for the while the United States should follow a "hands-off-Hawaii" policy.

Meanwhile Dole and his "P.G.'s," as they were called, went ahead improving conditions in the Islands. They worked to repeal the opium and lottery laws, to set up a National Guard, and to pass an act providing for a constitutional convention.

This last effort was designed to pave the way for the birth of the Republic of Hawaii.

Eighteen elected delegates—these included five native Hawaiians—met on May 30, 1894, and drafted a constitution which after many changes was adopted on July 3. This document gave a framework for a good administration which would serve until such time as Hawaii would be annexed by the United States. The Republic of Hawaii, proclaimed on the Fourth of July, was soon recognized by all the foreign powers with which Hawaii had relations.

Sanford B. Dole—his long, white, forked beard made him look much older than his fifty years—was the first and only President of the Republic. His ideals were high and he now had a chance to show what a sound government, based on American principles, could do for the Island people. But many knotty problems faced him. One soon led to open fighting.

After an uneasy six months, the royalists made a final effort to put Liliuokalani back on the throne by force. The police of the Republic believed that the royalists were trying to land guns and ammunition and to capture Honolulu. It was strange that the American warship *Pennsylvania* had sailed out of the harbor, leaving no American troops near the island of Oahu for the first time in twenty years. Was the expected counter-revolution at hand?

Near nightfall on Sunday, January 6, 1895, a telephone call led the police to inspect a house near Diamond Head. From a nearby canoe shed some shots rang out, and Charles L. Carter, who had joined the group to lend his help, fell with a fatal ball in his breast. He was the first victim of an outbreak of fighting that was the most serious since the days of Kamehameha I.

Evening services in Central Union Church were broken up when a messenger arrived with the word that the revolutionists had dug up hidden rifles on the beach and were marching on the town. Men poured out of the church and soon a citizens' guard patrolled the streets. Martial law was declared. Artillery was set up in Kapiolani Park, and shells from these guns and from a tug cruising off Diamond Head drove the rebel forces inland. Leader of the last stand was Robert W. Wilcox, who had led the revolt in the days of Kalakaua. He was captured several days later hiding in a fisherman's hut.

The Republic's police officers arrested about two hundred people for taking part in the uprising, including former Queen Liliuokalani. A small arsenal of arms and dynamite bombs was found in Washington Place, her spacious downtown home.

All the prisoners were tried for treason or lesser offenses, and nearly all were found guilty. Heavy sentences were imposed to show that revolution was no longer a game. But President Dole was merciful and used his pardoning power so widely that within a few months even the ringleaders were free. Liliuokalani signed a formal abdication and swore to uphold the Republic. But other problems still awaited President Dole's judgment and action.

One of these was to make sure that the Islands kept abreast of the age of modern invention. The city of Honolulu was no longer a sleepy Pacific town. The streets were lighted by electricity instead of kerosene lamps. People could ride on a mule-drawn street railway, foreshadowing an electric-railway line that would start in 1900. The fire department boasted steam-powered fire engines.

Telephones had been used in Hawaii only two years after Alexander Graham Bell took out the first patent. "Telephones are probably more numerous here," wrote a Honolulan in 1889, "than in any city in the United States with a like number of inhabitants." By 1898 there were thirteen hundred telephones on the island of Oahu alone.

Hawaii had issued its first stamp under the Postal Union in 1882 and seven years later began a parcel-post delivery under an agreement with the United States. In that same year, 1889, the first section of an undersea telegraph cable was laid between Maui and Molokai. Messages by Marconi radio could be sent among the Islands at the turn of the century, and by 1902 the Pacific cable from San Francisco would bring the world's tidings to Honolulu breakfast tables.

Roads had been improved and bridges built. In 1888 the right to build the first railway had been issued. By the time Dole became President of the Republic, narrow-gauge railways, used mainly for hauling sugar cane and other freight, were in operation not only on Oahu but on Maui and Hawaii, snaking through the fields or crossing deep gulches on spider-web trestles.

"Boat day" was still a gala occasion. News of a ship in the offing was telephoned to town by "Diamond Head Charlie," whose job was to watch for such an event from his cottage on the old crater. Many of the townsfolk would hurry to the wharf to greet the arriving passengers with flower *leis* and hear the latest news from the rest of the world.

Shipping had boomed. Things had changed since the period when the bulky old steamer *Kilauea* shuttled back and forth among the island ports for seventeen years. By 1890 no fewer than fourteen steamships, large and small, were running regularly on the interisland service.

Many big vessels were required to haul thousands of tons of sugar to market. Not all of these cargoes went in steamers; it was still possible to see in the harbor of Honolulu the tall masts of square-rigged clippers.

Honolulu was linked by regular shipping lines to many countries. After the Civil War the American Congress had authorized payment for a monthly mail-steamer service be-

tween San Francisco and Honolulu. A similar line connecting
with it ran south to Australia and New Zealand. In the 1880's,
Claus Spreckels started a semimonthly service between San
Francisco and Honolulu. Tourists from the United States and
many other countries could quite comfortably take ship and
visit the colorful island Republic in search of sunshine, health,
and fun.

Many other people had flocked to Hawaii, but not as
tourists. Perhaps the biggest problem of President Dole, aside
from obtaining annexation by the United States, was the immigration question.

A government Bureau of Immigration had been founded in
1864. Some of the plantation owners had disliked the use of
"coolie hands." One of the aims of King Kalakaua's trip
around the world had been to seek new sources of plantation
labor. India and Malaya were considered and rejected. In 1876
the bureau started encouraging people living in the Madeira
Islands in the Atlantic Ocean off Africa to emigrate to
Hawaii. The first shipload of these Portuguese islanders arrived two years later. They fitted in well, and by the end of
the century eighteen thousand of them had settled in Hawaii,
mostly as skilled workers on the plantations.

The cost of bringing laborers from Europe was high,
though, and it seemed that Asia must be the best place to seek
the larger numbers demanded by the boom after the reciprocity treaty was signed. In the later years of the century, the
chief source was the island kingdom of Japan.

A small band of laborers had been brought from Japan to
Hawaii in 1868, but thereafter no more arrived until 1885.
Then the influx of Japanese workers became a torrent. In 1894
the American Congress passed a new sugar act which was
again favorable to Hawaii. After that date, companies were set
up in Japan to bring shiploads of workers into Hawaii. Some

people were fearful that soon Hawaii might become a Japanese colony. By 1896, two years after the Republic began, one person in four living in the islands was Japanese.

It was feared that, if Hawaii was annexed, the American government would not allow further immigration into the Islands from Asia. Ship after ship poured newcomers into Honolulu. Toward the end of the Republic more than half the population was foreign-born. Thus a large population of workers was assured for Island employers when annexation was at last achieved. But President Dole had some trouble clearing the claims of the Japanese government before reaching his goal.

The annexationists headed by Dole had their hopes raised in 1896 when a Republican President was elected to go to Washington. A new treaty was quickly signed by both countries, but still Congress was slow to act. The sponsors of the Hawaii annexation bill decided to use a method that had worked for the admission of Texas into the Union. This was a joint resolution, which would require only a simple majority in each house of Congress. The resolution was introduced in the spring of 1898.

Something happened to sway the Congress at that time. This was the outbreak of the American war with Spain. On May Day, Admiral Dewey's fleet was victorious over the Spanish squadron in Manila Bay in the western Pacific. American troops were rushed to support Dewey. Hawaii might easily have remained neutral, but President Dole offered America "the unreserved alliance of Hawaii." Honolulu threw open its harbor to transports filled with American soldiers on their way to the Philippines. The lads were given a Hawaiian welcome.

It was clear that such a base as Pearl Harbor would become of high value in the Pacific in future. That argument turned the tide in favor of annexation. The two houses of Congress acted by July 6, and President McKinley signed the resolution the next day. The great news reached Honolulu on July 13. At last the fortunes of Hawaii and the United States would be forever linked!

The Republic of Hawaii turned over its powers during a brief ceremony on August 12. On a platform on the steps of Iolani Palace, President Dole and his cabinet met with the United States minister and officials of the Army and Navy. Thousands of citizens and foreign observers were there, but a number of Hawaiians stayed away out of respect for their former Queen.

The minister presented a copy of the joint resolution to white-bearded Dole, who then delivered to him the sovereignty of the Republic of Hawaii. At a signal just before noon, the Hawaiian flag was lowered to the strains of "Hawaii Ponoi." American banners broke out from the three towers of the palace and from the Judiciary Building across the street, while shore batteries and the U.S.S. *Philadelphia* boomed out a twenty-one-gun salute. The Hawaiian Islands were now a part of the American Union.

Hawaii, Territory of the U.S.A.

ALTHOUGH HAWAII WAS A PART OF THE UNITED STATES IN 1898, the new form of government for it was worked out slowly. For two years longer, Sanford Dole and his fellow officials carried on quite well.

The worst crisis they had to face was a terrible outbreak of bubonic plague. In the final days of the nineteenth century several fatal cases of this disease were reported in Honolulu. All schools were at once closed, and gatherings, even church services, were forbidden.

Most of the cases were found in a slum which had grown up in Honolulu, called Chinatown. Various methods of control were tried, including extermination of rats. The doctors were not quite sure of the connection between rats and the "Black Death," but they decided that the disease lurked in dirty dwellings. As a drastic attack on the plague, they ordered that the worst parts of Chinatown be burned down.

The fire department was put in charge and began burning infected sections. But on January 20, 1900, when they started firing one block, a rising wind carried sparks out of bounds. The flames reached supplies of kerosene and a shop full of firecrackers. Explosions roared. Soldiers ran to help fight the spreading fires and to lead fearful residents to safety. Miraculously no lives were lost. Before night, though, thirty-eight acres of houses in the downtown region had burned to ashes and more than four thousand persons were homeless.

This fiery purge did not wipe out the plague, which kept the port under quarantine for months more. Seventy persons died, and the loss of property and business, as well as the cost of fighting the disease, was high. One good result, though, was to call attention to the fact that sanitary and decent living conditions must be extended to all members of the community if any were to be safe.

This severe initiation was a prelude to the admission of Hawaii into the United States, on June 14, 1900, as an incorporated territory. Sanford B. Dole was appointed the first governor, and the Organic Act went into effect. This was the act of Congress which set up the government under which Hawaii was to operate for almost sixty years.

The Territory was governed upon a plan comparable to that of most states. There were, however, differences. To begin with, Congress, since it had created the Territory, could at any time abolish it or replace it with some other form, such as commission rule or even a military domination. Congress also could change any law passed by the territorial legislature, although as it turned out this right was never once used.

Under the Organic Act the governor and the secretary of the Territory were appointed by the President of the United

States, who also named all judges of higher courts. The governor appointed the heads of the various territorial departments, with the approval of the territorial senate. The legislature consisted of two houses, the senate and the house of representatives, both elected by the people. One delegate to Congress, also elected by the people, was a member of the United States House of Representatives. He could introduce bills but he had no vote on any bill.

All persons who had been citizens of Hawaii at the time of annexation became citizens of the United States. Thus the ordinary people in the Islands were granted more political power than they had ever before enjoyed. For more than twenty years the Hawaiians and part-Hawaiians formed a majority of the electorate, and for still another decade they outnumbered any other racial group of voters. Thus, those of Hawaiian blood for many years dictated the choice of men who sat in the territorial legislature.

At first this democratic power went to the heads of some of the legislators who met in the remodeled Iolani Palace to pass laws for Hawaii. The national pattern had been followed at once in the forming of Republican and Democratic parties in the Islands. But a third party also campaigned, the Home Rule party, with its slogan, "Hawaii for the Hawaiians." The first delegate to Congress was elected by this group. He was Robert W. Wilcox, who had twice led revolutions in the Islands. The same party also won a majority in each house of the first legislature, which wasted so much time in trifling debates that it came to be known as the "Lady Dog Legislature," because for the first twenty-four days it discussed a proposed tax on female dogs.

Soon, however, the legislators learned to avoid reckless leadership and to concern themselves more with statesmanship. Their record on the whole compares favorably with those won by the legislatures of most American states. The second delegate elected was Jonah Kuhio, nephew of Queen Liliuokalani, nicknamed "Prince Cupid," who continued to serve outstandingly in Washington until his death in 1922.

Governor Dole, whose term ended in 1903, finished at that time a decade in which he had been at the head of the government in Hawaii and had led the people from revolution through annexation to territorial rule under American democratic principles. He was followed by a succession of a dozen governors who supervised the slow change from outworn monarchy to practical democracy. The legislature handled many puzzling problems. They aimed at building a sound edifice in this Pacific laboratory of Americanism.

County governments similar to those on the mainland were created early in the century. The Oahu County government in 1907 was replaced by an administration for the "City and County of Honolulu," which included the entire island of Oahu. Honolulu is the biggest county in the world, for its boundaries run northwest for a thousand miles, nearly to Midway Island. Most of its area, however, is empty ocean.

These new governments cost more money, and Hawaii no longer could collect import revenues for territorial needs. In 1901 an income-tax law was passed, a successful experiment long before the federal amendment to the Constitution came in 1913. For many years the people of Hawaii paid all the usual federal taxes paid by mainland citizens, but often the Islanders did not get back from Washington the same benefits. "Taxation without representation" came to be one of the watchwords of those who felt that Hawaii would never get equal rights until it became a state.

"Americanization" was the slogan after Hawaii was annexed. Many people said that this goal could not be won, because so much of the population had come from Asia and because there was no large class of small farmers tilling their own lands. The Oriental aliens were barred by law from becoming American citizens, but their children born in the Islands were citizens under the Organic Act. Could these people be made Americans in spirit as well?

The ancestors of most mainland Americans had come from Europe, and it seemed that the only solution in Hawaii would be to bring there many settlers of European or mainland stock. It was assumed that they would get homesteads and set up small farms. But efforts to get lots of people to come to Hawaii from the States and set up replicas of Kansas homesteads never came to pass. More success came in settling native Hawaiians on homesteads; today some four thousand such families live on their own small holdings.

Higher hopes were held for quicker Americanization by bringing in people from European countries. The census of 1900, right after annexation, showed that Japanese comprised almost two fifths of the entire population of 154,000 people. Hawaiians and part-Hawaiians were about one fourth; Chinese, about one sixth; and Portuguese, about one eighth. Less than half the group were American citizens and less than 5 per cent were of Anglo-Saxon blood.

A new Board of Immigration, backed by the sugar planters, encouraged further importation of workers. Some came from Portugal, Spain, Puerto Rico, and even Russia, but few stayed long.

Asia and the Pacific were still the best hunting grounds for immigrants. Early in the century people started coming from Korea; their children and grandchildren are active in community life in Hawaii today. At about the same time a few families were brought from the Philippine Islands. Since then many thousands of Filipinos have made their homes in Hawaii.

The largest share of immigrants continued to come from

Japan. The inflow of Japanese men was checked by a so-called "gentlemen's agreement" between the American and Japanese governments in 1907. But "picture brides"—wives brought in through long-distance marriages—continued to come until the Immigration Act of 1924 excluded Orientals. The Japanese group was large enough to form a close colony, and retained its customs for a long while. Kimono wearers could be seen on the streets until World War II broke out.

After the attack on Pearl Harbor, the vast majority of "Americans of Japanese ancestry," as they liked to call themselves, were loyal to America and threw their efforts strongly into the fight for democracy. Like other immigrants, the Japanese were not always willing to remain as day laborers on plantations, but branched out into other occupations. Their children went through American schools, and today they are found in every branch of Hawaiian life, up to the highest positions in business, the professions, and politics.

Americanization of Hawaii did not come mainly through homesteading or through bringing immigrants from the States or Europe. Yet most people who know about modern Hawaii agree that it is a truly American community in every way that matters. The achievement of statehood by a territory more than two thousand miles off the American coast, and inhabited for the most part by people of Asian and Pacific ancestry, shows that American democracy will work in places other than North America, and with folk who did not come from Europe or New England.

The Island melting pot has truly welded people of a dozen national stocks into a new sort of American, with an attitude of tolerance not found anywhere else in the world. Over the years, these people of different races intermarried, and so did their children. Children in a schoolroom may show several dozen different combinations of racial background. A handsome lad who boasts English-Chinese-French-Korean ancestry may sit next to a lovely girl coming from Hawaiian-Japanese-Irish-Filipino stock. Young Hawaiians today—alert, healthy, smiling—lack hatred for those whose skin is a bit darker than theirs, or for those whose grandfathers once lived in Asia or on a South Pacific island. They are all good Americans together.

The influence of America on the Islands goes back a long way. There were Americans in Hawaii even before the United States had won its freedom from England. Since then, the Island people have become slowly more and more American in their ideals. Back in 1864, President Abraham Lincoln wrote of the Hawaiian kingdom: "Its people are free, and its laws, language, and religion are largely the fruit of our own teaching and example."

American schoolteachers and schools of American types have had much to do with this process, ever since the days of the New England missionaries who came to the court of Kamehameha II. Other agencies have been at work, too—churches, libraries, the Y.M.C.A. and Y.W.C.A., Boy Scouts and Girl Scouts, clubs and social groups of many kinds. Athletic sports and contests have also helped. On teams in the Islands, boys and girls of many racial backgrounds learned to work together and to respect each other's personalities and keen sportsmanship. But perhaps the strongest influence for Americanization has been the schools.

Ten years before annexation, a steady advance was begun toward the American ideal of public education. All English-language government schools were by 1888 free to students without the payment of tuition. American textbooks had by then been used in the schools for years, and 40 per cent of the teachers were Americans. Under the Republic, English was made the required classroom language. The Honolulu Normal and Training School was set up in 1896 to produce skilled teachers. Secondary education was begun with the founding of Honolulu High School in 1895.

The public schools had achieved such a high standard by 1900 that the framers of the Organic Act provided that no change need be made in the system. During the period of territorial rule, enrollment expanded many times, but the schools were kept up to date. Today a fifth of the money collected from all taxes is spent on public education.

Private schools have also continued to grow. About a hundred and fifty of them are found in the Islands, ranging from preschool through college. Punahou School, which has been turning out scholars for more than a century, is probably the best for college preparatory courses. Two schools begun by the Anglican Church under the monarchy—Iolani School for boys and St. Andrew's Priory for girls—are still thriving. An extensive Roman Catholic system has grown up, which includes St. Louis College for boys and Sacred Heart Academy for girls. The heavily endowed Kamehameha Schools, set up under the estate of Bernice Pauahi Bishop to educate boys and girls of Hawaiian blood, offer training from preschool through high school. A noted private high school is Mid-Pacific Institute, the successor of several Protestant schools which merged early in the twentieth century.

Four institutions of higher learning are found in the Islands. These are Honolulu Christian College (Protestant), Chaminade College (Catholic), Church College at Laie (Mormon), and the state-supported University of Hawaii.

The University of Hawaii was organized under another name in 1907; it was first termed a university in 1920. It lies at the mouth of Manoa Valley, three miles from the center of Honolulu and two miles from Waikiki Beach. It is open to all qualified students regardless of sex, racial ancestry, or national-ity. Its courses, which include not only those for the bachelor degrees but also those for Master of Arts and Doctor of Philosophy in a number of specialties, are recognized by other American universities. It also operates a junior college in the city of Hilo on the Big Island. Each summer more than a thousand students from the mainland fly to Honolulu to obtain credits and enjoy Hawaii as registrants in the university's celebrated summer session.

Student life on the "Rainbow Campus" differs little from that of college people everywhere. The university has an energetic all-year athletic program, and its teams compete in football, track, and water sports with various colleges in the other states. About a fourth of the regular student body is of Caucasian ancestry, but the rest reflects the complexion of the citizenry of the Fiftieth State, including such stocks as Japanese, Chinese, Hawaiian, Korean, Filipino, Puerto Rican, Samoan, and various intermixtures thereof. Students are proud of their colorful origins, and on festival days present bright pageants and dances which recall customs found in many parts of the Pacific and its borders. More and more, the University of Hawaii is becoming a truly international campus, with students from many countries, but especially from Asia. It will continue to act importantly as a center of knowledge in the Pacific, the ocean of America's future.

Prosperity at the Pacific Crossroads

THE FIRST AUTOMOBILE EVER SEEN IN HAWAII, ON A TRIAL SPIN in October, 1899, reached the startling speed of fourteen miles an hour.

Early in 1900 about twenty electric autos were brought in to be used as taxis, but the company went broke, and the cars lay rusting in the weeds because nobody could find use for them. The Chinese in town called automobiles "devil dragons." The cars frightened animals and children as they raced along at ten miles an hour. People still preferred the horse and carriage; automobiles either exploded or else broke down and had to be towed.

But in spite of this bad start, other automobiles were shipped to Hawaii. Today there are so many that the entire population could be put in the passenger cars that crowd the roads.

The highways of Oahu have highly civilized overpasses and traffic jams. On them one may see the license plates of all the other forty-nine states of the Union.

Large steamship lines grew up in the twentieth century to serve the increasing needs of Hawaii. In the early years, more than half the raw sugar crop was hauled the long distance around the bottom of South America to refineries on the eastern seaboard of the United States. Two lines owed their origins mainly to this trade. One was the Matson Navigation Company, founded in 1901. The other was the American-Hawaiian Steamship Company, which between 1900 and 1914 constructed twenty-two steel cargo vessels suitable for freighting sugar. These ran regularly between Honolulu and New York by way of the Strait of Magellan. These steamers cut in half the records of the sailing ships.

The Panama Canal was a boon to Pacific shipping. The first cargo to pass through the Canal was a bargeload of Hawaiian sugar in May, 1914, even before the route was formally opened.

Matson began catering to the passenger trade between the West Coast and Honolulu when in 1910 the little ship *Wilhelmina* began the run, foreshadowing the big white liners *Lurine* and *Matsonia* which nowadays deliver hundreds of tourists to Honolulu each month. Many round-the-world cruise ships put in at Hawaii, and Honolulu is connected by sea with all the other main ports of the globe.

Hawaii has become a crossroads of the sky as well as of the sea. The first air flight in the Islands was made by a civilian when, on the last day of 1910, Bud Mars took off from a polo field. Early aviators such as Tom Gunn, a Chinese, barnstormed in 1913 on several of the Islands, doing stunts.

Military aviation began in 1917, when the Army opened a flying center. When the value of air power was shown in

World War I, bases were set up by both Army and Navy to protect Oahu.

The Armed Forces pioneered in transoceanic flying. Two Navy planes under the command of John Rodgers made in September, 1924, the longest one-day flight up to that time when they took an admiral on an inspection tour from Honolulu to Hilo and back.

The following year, Rodgers headed the first flight from the West Coast to Hawaii. Three Navy seaplanes started on August 31, 1925, but two had to turn back, while Rodgers and his companions in the *PN 9-1* pushed on over the open ocean.

Naval ships were stationed a hundred miles apart along the route, and all seemed well. Then the radio of the *PN 9-1* fell silent, and for nine days nothing was heard of its crew. Later it was found that they had almost made the Islands in twenty-four hours. Then they had run out of gas two hundred miles short of Pearl Harbor and lacked power to operate their radio.

They floated in their seaplane for nine days, drifting toward the northwest. By burning wood from the edges of the lower wings, they managed to distill drinking water from the sea. They were sought by planes and surface vessels all this time, but it was a submarine that at last spotted the seaplane floating off Kauai. The *PN 9-1* was towed into a harbor on that island, and thus completed the first flight from California to Hawaii.

A few months after Charles Lindbergh flew the Atlantic alone, the first nonstop flight to Hawaii ended in the early morning of June 29, 1927, when two Army lieutenants, less than twenty-six hours out of Oakland, California, put down their trimotor monoplane, *Bird of Paradise*, at Wheeler Field on Oahu.

The first civilian flight ended with a crash landing when, on July 15 of the same year, Ernest L. Smith and Emory B.

Bronte, who had flown their monoplane for twenty-five hours, ran out of gas and plunged their craft into a clump of trees on Molokai, escaping unhurt.

A month later, a number of flyers taking part in "the first transoceanic flight race in history" were not so lucky. They were competing for two prizes offered by James D. Dole, then president of the Hawaiian Pineapple Company. Out of eight planes starting from Oakland on August 16, two smashed in taking off, two were forced to turn back, and two others disappeared in the Pacific. First in this longest overwater race up to that time was a monoplane piloted by Arthur C. Goebel. Second was Martin Jensen, the only Honolulan in the race. He and his navigator in the *Aloha* overshot Oahu and had to circle back, landing with only four gallons of gas in the tank. Altogether, the "Dole Derby," as it was called, cost the lives of ten persons—three in preparing for the flight, five during the race (one of them Mildred Doran, a girl flyer), and two in search efforts.

Air passenger service among the Islands began in 1929. Eight-seater amphibian biplanes were used, and the passengers were paddled out from the dock to the plane in outrigger canoes. Between runs, the planes were used for sightseeing over Oahu.

Hawaiian Airlines was the first United States line to operate daily freight deliveries, hauling all kinds of cargo among the Islands, including bulls, race horses, giant fish, and scenery for Hollywood movies made on island locations. Today this line and its rival, Aloha Air Line, provide more than fifty inter-island flights every day with clockwork regularity. People in Hawaii think no more of hopping a plane to another island than most people do about hopping a bus to the next city. Among the millions of passengers carried by the two lines through the years, not one rider or crewman has lost his life in an accident.

The trans-Pacific sky trail to the Orient was blazed in 1935 when the Pan-American China Clipper flew from the West Coast to Honolulu and on to Asia. Today, Honolulu International Airport is a roaring center for the eight scheduled trans-Pacific airlines that connect Hawaii with the other airports of the world. Honolulu is about four hours from San Francisco by jet plane, and something like eight hours from Washington, D.C. If necessary, Congressmen from Hawaii can get home on an overnight flight.

Raising crops has continued to be the mainstay of Hawaii's economy. Early in the century the cry was raised against concentrating on one or two types of crop. Efforts were made to start growing tea and rubber, and the raising of cotton, tobacco, and rice was revived. Recently, much income has been earned by growing gorgeous orchids (especially around Hilo on the Big Island) and other flowers, as well as toothsome macadamia nuts. But no other staple crop for bringing in market dollars can compare to sugar, pineapples, and coffee, the top products of Hawaii in the twentieth century.

Many kinds of harvests could be reaped on Hawaii's fields, but labor costs there are among the highest in the world. Crops requiring much handwork are ruled out. Other problems arise as well. To begin with, cultivable land amounts to no more than 7 per cent of the total area of the islands. On this land it was found impossible to grow both "money crops" and crops to furnish the usual food needs of the population. Concentrated tilling of this land for sugar and pineapples brings money to Mr. and Mrs. Hawaii with which they can buy supplies raised more cheaply in other regions. Hawaii spends each year about $800,000,000 for goods imported from the mainland states.

Growing of sugar and pineapple, then, for many years has

been the main way in which Hawaiian sunshine is transformed into payroll dollars. The two crops go well together. Sugar grows on lower lands where irrigation may be supplied; pineapples grow higher, on arid land, since they do not need much water.

Raising sugar and pineapples can scarcely be called farming in the usual sense. Both demand widespread operations and production through "factories in the fields." Both need all the latest discoveries of science and engineering for economical operation. There are few "homesteads"—only about a tenth of the sugar cane is grown on small holdings, and most of the growers send the cane to big mills for grinding. Operations must be on a large scale. To get one ton of sugar, seven to twelve tons of cane must be run through the mill. Since it takes two years to grow a sugar crop, much money must be invested ahead of time. The equipment needed for efficient handling is also very expensive. Raising cane in Hawaii is surely big business.

Scientific research has been the salvation of the sugar growers. The Hawaiian Sugar Planters' Association started an experiment station which spends about $2,000,000 a year to improve the industry. Much more than that sum is returned in savings through discoveries or improvements. Nowadays as much as a hundred tons of cane can be grown on one acre, yielding as much as fourteen tons of raw sugar. This high yield is important, because all the million-ton crops of recent years have been grown on only 200,000 acres—less than the area of New York City.

The research program has also shown great results in the use of soils, fertilizers, land, and water. Weeds are controlled by chemicals. The battle to protect the juicy green leaves of the plant from insect enemies has been fought for many years. For example, a tiny leaf hopper sneaked into the fields around 1900 and within four years had chewed up $3,000,000 worth of cane. Could a creature be found that was a natural enemy of the hopper? After long research, two scientists found in Australia another insect that laid its eggs in the body of the pest. Similarly, a wasp was brought from the Philippine Islands to control a beetle whose offspring grew fat by chewing the root systems of the cane stalk.

To keep down insects, large toads that even enjoy eating scorpions and centipedes were brought in from Puerto Rico in 1932. These ugly but hungry toads have done much to keep down the bug population.

Raising sugar has been the main industry of Hawaii for more than a century. For twenty-five years the annual crop has run over a million tons, and brings an income to the Islands of about $150,000,000. The twenty thousand employees are the highest-paid year-round agricultural workers in the world. More and more, huge machinery has replaced backbreaking human labor in the fields and mills. Improvements have enabled the sugar industry to turn out the same tonnage today as it did ten years ago, with only 60 per cent as many workers. Nobody is sorry.

If sugar is king in Hawaii, pineapple is queen. The crop value has risen in this century from almost nothing to more than $100,000,000.

Nobody knows who brought the first pineapple to Hawaii. Marín the Spaniard early experimented with them. During the gold rush some local pineapples were shipped to California, but the fruit went bad even when shipped green. Around 1884 an Englishman imported a thousand slips of the Smooth Cayenne variety from Jamaica. These are the grandparents of the cannery types of today's commercial pineapple.

The new variety spoiled in shipment even more quickly than the old. Canning was tried in 1892, but the difficulties seemed too great. The cans sometimes exploded on the wharves, aboard ship, and even on grocers' shelves.

After annexation, when American customs duties were no longer charged on Hawaiian fruit, a band of farmers from southern California settled around the town of Wahiawa in the middle of the island of Oahu. They grew several kinds of crops, including pineapples. The problem of saving hand labor was solved by planting the prickly rows of "pines" with seven-foot lanes between them, so that horse-drawn machinery could be used for cultivation. One day they hauled an abandoned cannery from Pearl Harbor and set it up at Wahiawa, where they began new experiments in preserving the fruit.

A leader in the new industry was James D. Dole, a distant relative of Sanford Dole, who had come from Boston in 1899. He started the Hawaiian Pineapple Company, one of the several large packers in operation today. Their plant near Honolulu is now the largest fruit cannery in the world, a favorite touring spot for thousands of visitors each year.

The first million-case pack was attained in 1912. Ten years later, the Hawaiian Pineapple Company bought nearly all the land on the island of Lanai and developed a harbor, a model town for the workers, and a barge line by which to ship the fruit to Honolulu.

Many of the procedures used by the pineapple growers were borrowed from the sugar industry. Again science has helped to make the work more efficient. A million dollars is spent each year by the Pineapple Research Institute, which among other things has found methods to keep down plant pests. Tarred mulching paper was an idea borrowed from the sugar growers. Young plants are started in holes made in yard-wide paper carpets whose use controls weeds, holds soil moisture, and retains warmth.

The ingenious "Ginaca" machine invented in 1913 handles

a hundred pineapples a minute in the cannery. It cuts off the shell and removes the core, leaving a smooth cylinder of yellow fruit ready to be sliced and canned. Even the harvesting is done by machines, which pass down the rows and fill giant bins with fruit that is cut, trimmed, and tossed on a conveyor belt by walking men armed with large knives.

Hawaii has about 73,000 acres covered with pineapple fields, whose terraced rows of spiky clumps are overburdened at harvest time with green-and-gold globes of ripe fruit. Hawaii still supplies three fourths of the world's needs for canned pineapple. Between three and four hundred million pineapples are picked annually. Many of the harvest workers are young people earning money for high school and college expenses. In addition to about thirty million cases of canned fruit and juice, many tons of fresh pineapples are shipped each year to the dinner tables of America. Nothing is wasted in the cannery. The process reclaims citric acid, alcohol, and natural sugar. Even the shell is made into fodder for cattle.

Income from the fields of sugar cane and pineapples that spread over the hills of Hawaii will be the lifeblood of its economy for years to come. The Islanders are happy to fill your sugar bowl and brighten your fruit cocktail.

Hawaii Becomes the Fiftieth Star

THE TWENTIETH CENTURY WAS FOR HAWAII NOT ONLY AN AGE of Americanization and progress. It was also a period when two world wars and other conflicts proved the value of the Islands as the Pacific fortress of the United States and a future state of the Union.

The population trebled under American rule. The need to protect the new territory early led to the building of Army and Navy bases in the islands. Ever since annexation, soldiers, sailors, and marines have been a familiar part of the picture in Hawaii.

The first permanent military post was Fort Shafter on the edge of Honolulu, still an important headquarters. Other forts were set up, ringing the city's harbor and Pearl Harbor to the west. Schofield Barracks, which finally grew to be the largest permanent Army post under the American flag, was first occupied in 1909.

The development of Pearl Harbor as a great naval base was begun after 1908. The channel between the ocean and the arms of the harbor was widened and deepened, and millions of yards of mud and coral were dredged out of the mooring areas inside. After much trouble, a gigantic dry dock was built on a coral foundation. Work was still going on when World War I broke out in Europe and spread to the Pacific.

World War I did not call for much naval action in Hawaiian waters. But almost a thousand men from the Islands served in the Army and Navy. People of all races and faiths joined in war work, contributed money and time to the American Red Cross, and labored on the home front. Many served in the war areas of Europe or Siberia, and the feeling grew that Hawaii was truly a part of America.

A generation later, World War II erupted. The Japanese air bombing of Pearl Harbor on December 7, 1941, plunged the United States into that war. The greatest defeat in American history aroused the battle spirit of Americans everywhere to muster, under the cry "Remember Pearl Harbor!", the greatest war power the world had yet known.

Smoke from the ruins of naval and air bases signaled to the people of Hawaii that they must dedicate themselves fully to a long struggle to aid their fellow Americans in the world fight against the powers of fascism.

The sneak attack of Japanese planes from a carrier force two hundred miles north of Oahu came early on that fatal Sunday morning. Bombers and torpedo planes struck Pearl Harbor and attacked most of the Pacific fleet, its battleships moored in a row. American planes were smashed on the ground near the harbor and at Schofield Barracks. Few planes ever got into the air to challenge the several hundred enemy aircraft that rained death from above.

The Japanese aerial torpedoes exploded as they hit the big battleships. Bombs crashed into the decks, ammunition magazines blew up, and several ships were blown on their sides by the force of the blasts. Only one or two ships managed to get under way before a second wave of dive bombers arrived to deal finishing strokes.

American naval power in the Pacific was crippled for many weeks after the smashing start of the war. All eight battleships in the harbor were put out of action. Three of them were repaired and restored to duty fairly soon, and three others, after terrific labor by hard-working shipyard men, were salvaged months later. Two others were total losses; the hull of the U.S.S. *Arizona*, tomb of eleven hundred sailors, is now a shrine for visitors to Pearl Harbor. Three cruisers were badly damaged, and three destroyers completely wrecked. Total American losses in killed, wounded, and missing were estimated at 3,435 men.

As radios in Honolulu blared, "Take cover! This is an attack!", the citizens of Hawaii rushed to help the stricken Armed Forces. The city was not a target, but random shells and fires caused by explosions cost the lives of sixty civilians on that "day of infamy," and about three hundred were wounded. This was the baptism of fire that made the people of Hawaii willing to face four years of heartbreaking battle in the Pacific.

They were ready, and continued to help in every way. Pearl Harbor, rebuilt and enlarged, became the staging area for the sea battles and island-hopping campaigns that at last led to the collapse of the fascist enemies in the Pacific. Hundreds of thousands of men and women of the Armed Forces passed through Hawaii or stayed to garrison these most strategic islands.

For the people of Hawaii, those were times of nightly blackouts, of martial law, of censorship; of bomb shelters, air-raid sirens, and gas masks for men, women, children, and babies; of barbed-wire barricades on lovely beaches. Except for the barehanded capture and killing of an armed Japanese aviator by a Hawaiian couple on the island of Niihau a week after the December 7 attack, there was no actual fighting on Hawaiian soil. At the end of that fatal month, Japanese submarines shelled, without much effect, ports on Hawaii, Kauai, and Maui.

Hawaii was a supply center, a prisoner-of-war area, and a rest and recreation region for war-weary men. Hawaiian hospitality was taxed to the utmost to cheer convalescents, entertain service folk with Honolulu Community Theater shows, and welcome them to churches, libraries, concert halls, and the Honolulu Academy of Arts.

The people of Hawaii contributed much more than their quota in war-bond purchases. They sought war jobs to supplement the labors of defense workers brought from the mainland. The chief task was to continue the agriculture of the Islands, since both sugar and pineapples were considered by the government to be essential crops. In almost all high schools the week was reduced so that students could volunteer for work in the fields.

The citizens of the Territory devoted themselves to winning the war, not only on the home front, but also through enlisting and serving far from their beloved islands. More than forty thousand men joined the Forces. By war's end, about two thousand men of Hawaii had been killed or permanently disabled in service. All branches of the Forces and every theater of action saw men and women from Hawaii. They represented all islands, all races, and every walk of life.

The loyalty of Hawaii's Japanese population in this war against Japan was clearly shown. Only a few of the Island Japanese were sent to the mainland as suspects. Fears of fifth-column activities turned out to be groundless. Later, Army and Navy officers testified to Congress that "not a single act of sabotage was committed by any resident of Hawaii before, during, or after the attack on Pearl Harbor." Far from plotting evil, many of the Japanese residents gave strong aid in the war, both at home and in distant lands.

Baseless fears by authorities kept most of the young Japanese men of military age out of the services for some months after the outbreak of the war. But when the Army decided to call for twelve hundred volunteers among the AJAs (Americans of Japanese ancestry, as they liked to call themselves), no fewer than ten thousand offered to enlist.

The war record of the 100th Infantry Battalion, made up mostly of AJAs from Hawaii, captured the imagination of America. In September, 1943, they fought their way ashore in Italy. Nine months later, having won fame as the "Purple Heart Battalion" because of their heavy battle losses, they were made a part of the newly arrived 442nd Regimental Combat Team, composed of AJA volunteers from the mainland United States as well as Hawaii. These soldiers fought so valiantly in the Italian and French campaigns that by V-E Day they were named by experts as "probably the most decorated unit in United States military history."

Other AJAs served in the Pacific fighting, often as interpreters, risking their lives at the front to intercept news of enemy movements. All in all, more than eighteen thousand Hawaiian men of Japanese blood served in the Armed Forces. No less than 80 per cent of those from Hawaii killed in the war and 88 per cent of those wounded were of Japanese ancestry. World War II unquestionably and favorably settled the question: Would people of many racial and national backgrounds—even Japanese—be strong fighters for American democracy during a war with Japan?

After the war was won—the celebration of V-J Day was the greatest spontaneous demonstration that the Islands had ever taken part in—another old question was again raised: Could Hawaii become a state of the Union?

The legislature had petitioned Congress for admission as a state as far back as 1903, and had made this request repeatedly after that. After World War I was over, statehood advocates felt that the Territory had grown up. The 1919 legislature adopted a memorial to Congress, pressing for statehood. At the same time, Delegate Jonah Kuhio introduced in Congress the first of a long succession of bills to grant statehood to Hawaii.

Most people realized that some time would have to pass before Congress granted this request. But they were bothered because many mainlanders, including congressmen, looked upon the Islands as a mere colony rather than as an incorporated territory only one stage removed from statehood. Hawaii was subject to all taxes imposed on the states, but was excluded from the benefits of federal laws giving appropriations for roads, schools, and many other improvements.

The legislature in 1923 enacted what was called "Hawaii's Bill of Rights," requesting the same treatment from Congress as that received by the individual states. Congress acknowledged the justice of this claim by passing in 1924 a law extending to Hawaii the benefits of previous appropriations. But the delegate still had to watch new bills to see that Hawaii was not left out.

At the same time the Island people were concerned about

the fact that they might be governed by appointed "carpet-baggers," who had never lived in the Territory and did not know its problems well. The Organic Act was amended in 1931 to make a three-year residence a requirement for appointment to most territorial and federal positions in Hawaii.

The Islanders were busy after 1929 trying to survive the bad economic depression of those years. Two things happened in the 1930's that made the people of Hawaii strongly aware that their position as a democratic community was not safe. One was an act of Congress in 1934 which discriminated against the sugar producers of the Territory. This unfair law made it clear that Congress could at any time, if it wished, take away almost all the rights of Hawaii's citizens.

Another source of worry was a murder in Honolulu which shocked the nation and led to cries that law was not well enforced there. After an investigation, the legislature passed new laws to correct any laxness. But for a time it was feared that Congress would take away all freedoms and perhaps set up a commission rule over Hawaii, under Army and Navy officers. These restrictive bills did not pass and home rule was saved for a while, but thoughtful citizens began to feel that a strong campaign for statehood should be started.

During the late 1930's, a number of congressional hearings were held, in the Islands and in Washington, concerning Hawaii's fitness for statehood. In 1937 one of these groups reported that Hawaii had "fulfilled every requirement for statehood heretofore exacted of territories." It suggested holding a vote to see whether the population desired statehood.

This question was put on the ballot in 1940. This was an unfavorable time, for a war against Japan was looming. Even so, the people of the Islands voted more than two to one in favor of statehood.

After World War II showed the democratic loyalty of the

Islanders, an even more firm campaign for statehood led to further hearings. In 1947, the House of Representatives of the Eightieth Congress approved a statehood bill by 197 to 133 and forwarded it to the Senate, but no favorable action was taken there.

In 1949 the Hawaii legislature decided to try another approach, which had been used by fifteen other territories that later became states. This was to draft a constitution which could go into effect as soon as an enabling act might be passed. On April 4, 1950, sixty-three delegates elected from most parts of the Island population began drafting a model constitution, which was later approved by the people.

An enabling act was passed by the House of Representatives in Washington in March, 1950. But the Korean War broke out a few months later, and Hawaii like the rest of the country was busily engaged in defending American rights in this new conflict in the Pacific. Toward the end of that year, opponents of the bills to grant statehood to Hawaii and Alaska forestalled a vote.

The supporters of Hawaiian statehood started over again, and fought to obtain victory in later sessions of Congress. In 1957, statehood failed to pass Congress for the twenty-second time since 1903. But the supporters did not lose hope. When in 1958 the Territory of Alaska was granted statehood, Hawaii's hopes rose. Sure enough, in 1959, an enabling act was passed by the Senate on March 11, by a vote of 76 to 15. Next day the House of Representatives concurred by an overwhelming vote of 323 to 89. President Eisenhower signed the act on March 18.

The law called for a vote by the people on whether they agreed to become citizens of the Fiftieth State. The vote on June 27 was seventeen to one in favor of statehood. On August 21, President Eisenhower proclaimed that a slate of congressmen and state authorities elected on July 28 should take office.

The first fifty-star flag would be flown on the following Fourth of July.

The long road had ended with Hawaii as a full member in the sisterhood of the Union. The lure of American ideals, which had started when some Americans visited Hawaii with Captain Cook, had been victorious. Hawaii would benefit, and the rest of America would benefit, too. As James A. Michener, noted author who had chosen to live in Hawaii, put it: "Those of us in Hawaii well appreciate what a bold step America has taken in extending statehood to the islands. That Congress chose to do so is a supreme joy to most of the islanders, and we are determined that America shall never regret that daring decision. And for its part, the United States today is a little stronger, a little more secure, a little more courageous."

PAU

Some Facts About Hawaii

A. THE STATE OF HAWAII

Capital. Honolulu, on the island of Oahu.

Population. Civilian, 1,055,700 (estimated 1989). Three fourths of the people live on the island of Oahu.

Nickname. Aloha State.

State Motto. Ua mau ke ea o ka aina i ka pono (The life of the land is preserved in righteousness).

State Flag. The British Union Jack appears in the upper-left-hand corner of the flag. The eight stripes of white, red, and blue represent the main islands of the group.

State Seal. The figure of King Kamehameha I stands on the right side of the coat of arms, and the Goddess of Liberty stands on the left, holding the state flag. The words "State of Hawaii" curve around the top of the seal, and the state motto appears at the bottom. The date 1959 indicates the year of admission into the Union. The shield has two quarters showing stripes of the state flag and two showing, on a yellow field, a white ball on a black staff. In the center is a small green shield with a five-pointed yellow star. Below is a phoenix rising from the flames, and clusters of taro and banana leaves and maidenhair fern.

State Tree. Kukui, or candlenut.

State Colors. Red and yellow.

Size. The eight largest islands cover 6,422 square miles, including 16 square miles of inland water. Coast line, 944 miles. Hawaii ranks forty-seventh among the states in land area.

Main Islands	Square Miles
Hawaii, "The Big Island"	4,021
Kahoolawe (uninhabited)	45
Kauai, "The Garden Isle"	551
Lanai, "The Pineapple Island"	141
Maui, "The Valley Isle"	728
Molokai, "The Friendly Island"	260
Niihau, "The Mystery Island"	72
Oahu, "The Gathering Place"	604

Government. Hawaii sends two senators and one representative to the United States Congress. A state constitution approved by the people in 1950 went into effect in 1959. The state legislature consists of twenty-five senators, elected for four-year terms, and fifty-one representatives, elected for two-year terms. A governor and a lieutenant-governor are elected for four-year terms. Not more than twenty principal departments of the state government are authorized, with heads appointed by the governor with the advice and consent of the state senate. The state is divided into five counties. Of these the largest is the City and County of Honolulu, which operates under a charter that went into effect in 1959. It is headed by a mayor and nine councilmen elected for four-year terms.

Voting. Qualifications include citizenship, registration, residence of one year in the state, attainment of the age of twenty years, and ability to speak, read, and write the English or Hawaiian language.

Courts. The state supreme court consists of a chief justice and four associate justices, appointed for four-year terms by the governor, with the advice and consent of the state senate. The governor also appoints four circuit-court judges for six-year terms.

Climate. Although the main islands lie inside the torrid zone, prevailing northeast trade winds keep them pleasantly cool, except for a few days each year when kona, or southerly winds, cause muggy weather and occasional downpours. Many varieties of climate may be found on the various islands since elevations range from sea level up to almost 14,000 feet on volcanic peaks which are snow-capped part of each year.

In most spots there is little difference in temperature between summer and winter or day and night. Average July temperature is about 80° F. and average January temperature about 65° F. Highest on record was 100° F. on the Big Island and lowest was 18° F. at Haleakala Crater. Honolulu average year-round temperature is 75° F., with record ranges of 90° and 56° F.

Rainfall varies from hundreds of inches a year on the mountaintops to less than ten inches in the lowlands. The heaviest rains generally fall on the northeastern sides of the islands, where the trade winds first touch the peaks. Mount Waialeale, on the island of Kauai, is one of the wettest spots in the world; it averages 476 inches of rain a year.

Chief Products. Hawaii produces about one eighth of the sugar used in the United States, and three fourths of the world's crop of commercial pineapples. Other agricultural products include coffee, cattle, chickens and eggs, dairy products, hogs, and flowers. Manufactured goods include sportswear, canned and frozen pineapple, fruit juices, and canned tuna.

Annual Events. In addition to all the regular American holidays (including a New Year's Eve brilliant with fireworks), Hawaii enjoys the following celebrations: January or February, Chinese New Year and Narcissus Festival (no fixed date). March 26, Kuhio Day, honoring one of Hawaii's first delegates to Congress. April or May, Cherry Blossom Festival (no fixed date). May 1, Lei Day. June 11, Kamehameha Day, honoring first king of united islands. July-August, Japanese Bon dances, at

Buddhist temples, every weekend. August, Hula Festival at Honolulu, first four Sundays. October, Aloha Week (no fixed date).

Other Facts. Hawaii is the southernmost American state, and the only one, except Alaska, not connected to continental United States. It is the only state composed solely of islands. It is the only one formerly an independent kingdom.

B. HEADS OF GOVERNMENT IN HAWAII

1. *Native Monarchs*

NAME	BIRTH	ACCESSION	DEATH
Kamehameha I	c. 1758	1795	May 8, 1819
Kamehameha II			
(Liholiho)	1797	May 20, 1819	July 14, 1824
Kamehameha III			
(Kauikeaouli)	March 17, 1814	June 6, 1825	Dec. 15, 1854
Kamehameha IV			
(Alexander Liholiho)	Feb. 9, 1834	Dec. 15, 1854	Nov. 30, 1863
Kamehameha V			
(Lot Kamehameha)	Dec. 11, 1830	Nov. 30, 1863	Dec. 11, 1872
William C. Lunalilo	Jan. 31, 1835	Jan. 8, 1873	Feb. 3, 1874
David Kalakaua	Nov. 16, 1836	Feb. 12, 1874	Jan. 20, 1891
Liliuokalani	Sept. 2, 1838	Jan. 29, 1891	Nov. 11, 1917

Liliuokalani was deposed and the Hawaiian kingdom came to an end on January 17, 1893.

2. *President of Provisional Government*

NAME	TERM BEGAN	TERM ENDED
Sanford B. Dole	Jan. 17, 1893	July 4, 1894

3. *President of Republic of Hawaii*

Sanford B. Dole	July 4, 1894	June 14, 1900

Hawaii was annexed to the United States on August 12, 1898, but the Territorial government was not established until June 14, 1900.

4. *Governors of Territory of Hawaii*

NAME	APPOINTED BY PRESIDENT	TERM ENDED
Sanford B. Dole	McKinley	Nov. 23, 1903
George R. Carter	T. Roosevelt	Aug. 15, 1907
Walter F. Frear	T. Roosevelt	Nov. 29, 1913
Lucius E. Pinkham	Wilson	June 22, 1918
Charles J. McCarthy	Wilson	July 5, 1921
Wallace R. Farrington	Harding	July 5, 1925
(second term)	Coolidge	July 5, 1929
Lawrence M. Judd	Hoover	March 1, 1934
Joseph B. Poindexter	F. D. Roosevelt	April 2, 1938
(second term)	F. D. Roosevelt	Aug. 24, 1942
Ingram M. Stainback	F. D. Roosevelt	Aug. 24, 1946
(second term)	Truman	April 30, 1951
Oren E. Long	Truman	Feb. 28, 1953
Samuel Wilder King	Eisenhower	Sept. 2, 1957
William F. Quinn	Eisenhower	Aug. 21, 1959

5. *Governor of State of Hawaii*

William F. Quinn	Elected July 28, 1959	Republican
John A. Burns	Elected November 6, 1962	Democrat
George R. Ariyoshi	Elected November 5, 1974	Democrat
John Waihee	Elected November 4, 1986	Democrat

C. HEADLINE HISTORY OF HAWAII, 1960-1990

1960. The seventh federal census shows the island population as 609,096. Congress authorizes the creation of the Center for Cultural and Technical Interchange between East and West (East-West Center) at the University of Hawaii; grantees come from all fifty states of the Union and from twenty-six countries of Asia and the Pacific to obtain advanced education in Hawaii and travel on the mainland. *February 18.* The state legislature convenes in its first regular session. It adjourns May 2. *May 23.* Devastating tsunami waves strike the islands and kill fifty-seven persons at Hilo; earthquakes rock the Puna district and an eruption pours lava on Kula subdivision. *July 4.* Hawaii's state flag becomes official and a fiftieth star is added to the American flag. *November.* The people of Hawaii have their first chance to vote for president of the United States; on a recount, John F. Kennedy wins over Richard Nixon by a margin of 115 votes out of 184,705. All three Congressional incumbents are re-elected.

1961. *April 20.* The first cable television service is offered by Kaiser-Teleprompter. *June 25.* The Conference of State Governors holds its annual meeting in Honolulu. *July 1.* The two sections of Hawaii National Park become separate entities, Hawaii Volcanoes National Park and Haleakala National Park; on the same day the National Park Service creates the City of Refuge National Historical Park at Kona.

1962. *November.* Governor Quinn is defeated by John R. Burns. Daniel K. Inouye joins Hiram L. Fong as the first Senate members of Oriental ancestry. Reapportionment brings two seats in the House, which are filled by two Democrats, Thomas P. Gill and Spark M. Matsunaga. For the first time in history, Democrats control both houses of the legislature.

1963. *June 9.* President John F. Kennedy addresses the National Conference of Mayors in Honolulu. The Polynesian Cultural Center opens as an attraction to visitors.

1964. An undersea cable costing $84,000,000 begins operation between Hawaii and Tokyo. *November.* Senator Fong is elected to a full six-year term. Congressman Matsunaga is re-elected, and Patsy Takemoto Mink becomes a member of the House.

1965. The Viet Nam conflict calls the 25th Division and the Marines to the Asian area. A proposed Kauai National Park arouses a mass of controversy. The state community-college system is created.

1966. *April 25.* The United States Supreme Court upholds Hawaii's reapportionment plan based on registered voters rather than population. *November 19.* Live television to and from the mainland is inaugurated.

1967. This becomes the first year during which one million tourists visit the islands. Hawaii Loa College is founded.

1968. Frank F. Fasi becomes mayor of the City and County of Honolulu for the first time, and the neighbor islands elect their first mayors. The legislature meets for the first time in the new Capitol building.

1969. *July 22.* The Civil Aeronautics Board awards domestic Pacific routes to seven airlines from Hawaii to thirty-five mainland cities. *July 26.* The first human beings returning from the moon, astronauts Neil A. Armstrong, Edwin E. Aldrin, Jr., and Michael Collins, arrive at Pearl Harbor aboard carrier *Hornet*, which had picked them up after splashdown of their Apollo 11 craft, *Columbia 3*.

1970. Eighth federal census records island population to be 769,913. Hiram L. Fong is re-elected to the Senate.

1971. Honolulu Rapid Transit, because of a labor dispute, is taken over by the City and County of Honolulu and operated as MTL, Inc. The University of Hawaii Law School is founded.

1972. Direct distance dialing permits callers to bypass long-distance operators on calls from Oahu to the rest of the world.

1973. *April 2.* Hawaii's teachers begin the nation's first statewide school strike in a dispute over pay and working conditions. *April 26.* Hilo suffers an earthquake causing $1,000,000 in damage. *September.* "Roll-on, roll-off" trailership is introduced by Matson Navigation Co. with two ships, *Lurline* and *Matsonia*. First annual Honolulu Marathon is run by 167 contestants.

1974. The forty-year-old sugar act expires and prices soar from 11 cents a pound to 65.5 cents. Hawaii becomes the first state to impose limits on the sale of gasoline during a world shortage; the ban is ended on April 30. *August 12-16.* The American Bar Association holds is 97th annual convention in Honolulu. *November 5.* George R. Ariyoshi is elected first governor of Oriental ancestry.

1975. *June 15.* Sea Flite makes its first scheduled inter-island passenger trip by hydrofoil with the 45-knot *Kamehameha*, but service is discontinued on January 15, 1978. Aloha Stadium is opened. KHVH radio becomes the first Hawaii station to regularly air twenty-four-hour programs from the mainland.

1976. Hawaii takes part in the national American bicentennial celebrations of the signing of the Declaration of Independence and carries out numerous projects. The sailing craft *Hokulea* makes a voyage to Tahiti and returns to recall the days of Polynesian canoe travel. Hawaiian activists begin efforts to release the island of Kaho'olawe from Navy use. *November.* Senators from Hawaii are Daniel K. Inouye and Spark M. Matsunaga and representatives are Cecil Heftel and Daniel K. Akaka, first Congressman of Hawaiian ancestry.

1977. *September 13.* The world's most active volcano, Kilauea, begins to erupt and continues intermittent outbursts until September 28. An 188-day strike begun by the Ironworkers' Union halts construction on projects throughout the state.

1978. Hawaii celebrates the bicentennial of the arrival of Captain James Cook and two British ships. *July 5.* The third constitutional convention since the first in 1950 is convened; a ninety-day session produces numerous proposals, all of which are ratified by voters in the November elections. *November 6.* George R. Ariyoshi wins a second term as governor and state senator Jean Sadako King becomes the first woman lieutenant governor in the history of the state.

1979. Despite a strike against United Airlines and grounding of DC-10 planes because of safety problems, almost four million visitors come to Hawaii. *October.* Many international dignitaries attend the dedication of one of the largest infrared telescopes in the world, joining other observatories atop Mauna Kea on the Big Island, where clear skies advance astronomical research. *October 21.* A forty-one-day strike by the lowest-paid unit of the United Public Workers begins and lasts until December 3. *November.* The fiftieth anniversary of inauguration of the first inter-island air service is celebrated.

1980. *November.* Eileen Anderson defeats Frank F. Fasi, mayor since 1968, to become the first woman to head the City and County of Honolulu. Charles Marsland is Honolulu's first elected prosecutor.

1981. The seventy-fifth anniversary of Filipino migration to the islands is celebrated. An eighty-year-old landmark, the Alexander Young Hotel in downtown Honolulu, is demolished to make way for increasing highrise development.

1982. *November.* George R. Ariyoshi defeats Republican Andy Anderson and Independent Frank F. Fasi for governor. *November 23.* Hurricane Iwa strikes Kauai with winds as high as 117 miles an hour, causing an estimated $24 million in damage. It is the most destructive storm to hit Hawaii in historic times.

1983. Official population of Hawaii reaches 1,083,000. Ethnic distribution: Caucasion, 24.5 per cent; Japanese, 23.2 per cent; Filipino, 11.3 per cent; Hawaiian and part-Hawaiian, 20.0 per cent. Kilauea Volcano spews lava on the Big Island, first phase of an island-building eruption that continues into the 1990's.

1984. Twenty-fifth anniversary of statehood is celebrated. Frank F. Fasi defeats Eileen Anderson to regain longtime mayoralty of the City and County of Honolulu. All four Congressional votes go to Ronald Reagan.

1985. Visitor count tops five million. Three Honolulu city councilmen are recalled for switching parties.

1986. *January 28.* Space Shuttle *Challenger* explodes after takeoff, killing the entire crew, including Hawaii's Ellison Onizuka. Corazon Aquino becomes president of the Republic of the Philippines; the Ferdinand Marcos family flees for asylum to live in Hawaii. *November.* John Waihee becomes the first person of part-Hawaiian ancestry to be elected governor.

1987. Polynesian sailing craft *Hokulea* completes a two-year "voyage of rediscovery" to demonstrate native navigation methods. "Ho'olako 1987"—the Year of the Hawaiian—is celebrated. Devastating storm on New Year's Eve causes wide damage.

1988. The Hawaiian Maritime Center opens on the waterfront as an oceanic museum and visitor attraction. Despite the closing of fourteen plantations out of twenty-seven in past years, production for 1988 reaches almost a million tons of raw sugar—about the same as in 1959—and yield per acre has increased by one third. *November.* Daniel K. Inouye, in Congress since 1962, is reelected. Spark M. Matsunaga, in the Senate since 1976, dies in office and Patsy Takemoto Mink is elected in his district. Daniel Akaka, in the House since 1976, is unopposed, and Patricia Saiki is elected. Almost unique among the states, Hawaii gives all four presidential votes to Michael Dukakis.

1989. Hawaii becomes the first state to outlaw chlorofluorocarbon refrigerants to help protect the earth's ozone layer.

1990. Kilauea Volcano is the longest-running uninterrupted performer on record, continuing destruction in Puna. *November.* Daniel K. Inouye is reelected to the Senate, and Neil Abercrombie and Patsy Takemoto Mink are elected to the House. John Waihee defeats Andy Anderson and is reelected governor. The state of Hawaii enters the last deciade of the twentieth century with a large, multi-ethnic population, a booming economy, and a strong confidence in facing its Pacific destiny.

Index

198

Key to Hawaiian Pronunciation

The Hawaiian language was first written by missionaries, using a Roman alphabet which is completely phonetic. All letters are pronounced.

The seven consonants—*h, k, l, m, n, p*, and *w*—are pronounced much as in English, except that the *h* is never silent. The *w* is either a lax English *w* or a very lax *v*. After *e* or *i*, almost all speakers use the *v* sound.

Vowels are *a, e, i, o*, and *u*, pronounced as in Latin or Spanish. There are no true diphthongs, but the following are roughly pronounced thus: *ae* and *ai* are like *ai* in the English "aisle"; *ao* and *au* like *ow* in "cow"; and *ei* like *ay* in "day."

Every syllable ends in a vowel, and many syllables contain only vowels. Most Hawaiian words are stressed on the next to the last syllable; some words have an even stress. The spoken language has a lilting, musical softness pleasing to the ear.

TALES OF THE PACIFIC

JACK LONDON
Stories of Hawaii $4.95
South Sea Tales $4.95
Captain David Grief (originally A Son of the Sun) $4.95
The Mutiny of the "Elsinore" $4.95

HAWAII
Remember Pearl Harbor by Blake Clark $4.95
Kona by Marjorie Sinclair $4.95
The Spell of Hawaii $4.95
A Hawaiian Reader $4.95
Russian Flag Over Hawaii by Darwin Teilhet $3.95
Teller of Tales by Eric Knudsen $4.95
Myths and Legends of Hawaii by W.D. Westervelt $4.95
Mark Twain in Hawaii $4.95
The Legends and Myths of Hawaii by Kalakaua $6.95
Hawaii's Story by Hawaii's Queen $6.95
Rape in Paradise by Theon Wright $4.95
The Betrayal of Liliuokalani $6.95
The Wild Wind by Marjorie Sinclair $4.95
Hawaii: Fiftieth Star by A. Grove Day $4.95
Hawaii and Its People by A. Grove Day $4.95
True Tales of the South Seas ed. by A. Grove Day and Carl Stroven $4.95

SOUTH SEAS LITERATURE
The Trembling of a Leaf by W. Somerset Maugham $3.95
The Book of Puka-Puka by Robert Dean Frisbie $3.95
The Lure of Tahiti, ed. by A. Grove Day $3.95
The Blue of Capricorn by Eugene Burdick $3.95
Horror in Paradise, ed. by A. Grove Day and Bacil F. Kirtley $4.95
Best South Sea Stories, ed. by A. Grove Day $4.95
The Forgotten One by James Norman Hall $3.95
His Majesty O'Keefe by Lawrence Klingman and Gerald Green $4.95

TRAVEL, BIOGRAPHY, ANTHROPOLOGY
Manga Reva by Robert Lee Eskridge $3.95
Coronado's Quest by A. Grove Day $3.95
Love in the South Seas by Bengt Danielsson $4.95
Home from the Sea: Robert Louis Stevenson in Samoa by Richard A.
    Bermann $3.95
The Nordhoff-Hall Story: In Search of Paradise by Paul L. Briand, $4.95
The Fatal Impact by Alan Moorehead $4.95
Claus Spreckels: The Sugar King in Hawaii by Jacob Adler $3.95
A Dream of Islands by Gavan Daws $4.95

Orders should be sent to Mutual Publishing Co.
1127 11th Ave. Mezz. B, Honolulu, HI 96816. Add $2.00
handling for the first book and $1.00 for each book
thereafter. For airmail add $3.00 per shipment.